TRADING SPACES

Foreign direct investments (FDI) are investments that multinational corporations make to produce goods and services in foreign countries. In this book, Professor Sonal S. Pandya studies how and why those foreign countries regulate FDI, including how citizens form policy preferences about FDI in their countries and how those countries regulate foreign ownership. Pandya argues that, in general, FDI raises labor demand and increases competition for the local firms in those foreign countries. In turn, country policy makers regulate FDI when, because of the country's political structure, they privilege the economic interests of local firms. This model implies that FDI regulation varies by country and industry type as a function of changes in how FDI affects the economic interests of labor and capital, as well as changes in policy makers' political incentives to regulate FDI. Pandya tests this theory with, among other things, an original dataset of foreign ownership regulations in more than 100 countries during the 1970–2000 period. In so doing, this book helps researchers better understand the economic and political foundations of global economic integration, as well as the economic conflicts between countries with advanced economies and countries with large emerging markets such as China and India.

Sonal S. Pandya is an Assistant Professor of Politics at the University of Virginia. She specializes in international relations with a focus on the interdisciplinary study of international political economy. Her research interests include the political economy of foreign direct investment, international politics and consumer behavior, and the global flow of intangible assets including intellectual property and skills. Professor Pandya received her PhD from Harvard University. This book is based on her doctoral dissertation for which she received the American Political Science Association's 2009 Mancur Olson Award for the Best Dissertation in Political Economy.

Political Economy of Institutions and Decisions

Series Editors
Stephen Ansolabehere, *Harvard University*
Jeffry Frieden, *Harvard University*

Founding Editors
James E. Alt, *Harvard University*
Douglass C. North, *Washington University of St. Louis*

Other Books in the Series

Alberto Alesina and Howard Rosenthal, *Partisan Politics, Divided Government, and the Economy*

Lee J. Alston, Thrainn Eggertsson, and Douglass C. North, eds., *Empirical Studies in Institutional Change*

Lee J. Alston and Joseph P. Ferrie, *Southern Paternalism and the Rise of the American Welfare State: Economics, Politics, and Institutions, 1865-1965*

James E. Alt and Kenneth Shepsle, eds., *Perspectives on Positive Political Economy*

Josephine T. Andrews, *When Majorities Fail: The Russian Parliament, 1990-1993*

Jeffrey S. Banks and Eric A. Hanushek, eds., *Modern Political Economy: Old Topics, New Directions*

Yoram Barzel, *Economic Analysis of Property Rights, 2nd edition*

Yoram Barzel, *A Theory of the State: Economic Rights, Legal Rights, and the Scope of the State*

Robert Bates, *Beyond the Miracle of the Market: The Political Economy of Agrarian Development in Kenya*

Jenna Bednar, *The Robust Federation: Principles of Design*

Charles M. Cameron, *Veto Bargaining: Presidents and the Politics of Negative Power*

Kelly H. Chang, *Appointing Central Bankers: The Politics of Monetary Policy in the United States and the European Monetary Union*

Peter Cowhey and Mathew McCubbins, eds., *Structure and Policy in Japan and the United States: An Institutionalist Approach*

Gary W. Cox, *The Efficient Secret: The Cabinet and the Development of Political Parties in Victorian England*

Gary W. Cox, *Making Votes Count: Strategic Coordination in the World's Electoral System*

Gary W. Cox and Jonathan N. Katz, *Elbridge Gerry's Salamander: The Electoral Consequences of the Reapportionment Revolution*

(continued after Index)

Trading Spaces

Foreign Direct Investment Regulation, 1970–2000

SONAL S. PANDYA
University of Virginia

CAMBRIDGE
UNIVERSITY PRESS

CAMBRIDGE
UNIVERSITY PRESS

32 Avenue of the Americas, New York, NY 10013-2473, USA

Cambridge University Press is part of the University of Cambridge.

It furthers the University's mission by disseminating knowledge in the pursuit of education, learning, and research at the highest international levels of excellence.

www.cambridge.org
Information on this title: www.cambridge.org/9781107040342

© Sonal S. Pandya 2014

First published 2014

Printed in the United States of America

A catalog record for this publication is available from the British Library.

Library of Congress Cataloging in Publication data
Pandya, Sonal S. Trading spaces : foreign direct investment
regulation, 1970–2000 / Sonal S. Pandya.
pages   cm. – (Political economy of institutions and decisions)
Includes bibliographical references and index.
ISBN 978-1-107-04034-2 (hardback)
1. Investments, Foreign.   2. Investments, Foreign–Political aspects.   I. Title.
HG4538.P35   2014
332.67′3–dc23   2013018645

ISBN 978-1-107-04034-2 Hardback

Contents

Figures

Tables

Preface and Acknowledgments

My interest in foreign direct investment (FDI) began, as much research does, with a naïve question: Why do countries restrict inward FDI? When I was a graduate student, the cutting-edge research in international political economy drew extensively from economics to derive testable claims about the political economy of international trade and monetary policy. FDI, however, was seldom mentioned. I had written my undergraduate thesis on telecommunications liberalization in the World Trade Organization, an area in which market access for multinational firms is a key issue. FDI seemed very important to global economic integration but it was strangely absent from the current political economy research. From my perspective as a third-year PhD student existing political economy theories of FDI were far from the cutting-edge research to which I aspired. So, motivated by my naïve question, I hatched an equally naïve plan: to study FDI the same way that everyone studies trade and money – that is, to develop and test explanations for countries' policies based on a rigorous account of FDI's economic consequences.

Now, nearly a decade later, I can report that there were very good reasons why political economy scholars had not studied FDI in this way. In order to do this research I had to confront two significant obstacles. First, there is no standard definition of FDI regulation, let alone readily available data on regulations. I had to pin down what exactly it means to restrict inward FDI and how to measure those restrictions. Second, I had to develop a tractable way of theorizing about FDI and its economic consequences. FDI encompasses virtually all industries from agriculture to advanced manufacturing to high-skill services like banking and law. There were no pithy economic models of FDI from which I could borrow. The challenge I faced was how to develop a theoretical framework that would produce meaningful insights across such a wide range of economic activities. As this book attests, I did eventually figure out how to address these obstacles. My naiveté turned out to be a blessing. I may not have pursued this research had I fully grasped these challenges at the outset.

While I think this book is a reasonably convincing answer to my initial question, the process of writing actually produced the more valuable rewards. It has changed how I think about international economic integration. In thinking about what makes FDI distinctive as a form of economic activity, I came to appreciate how the organization of economic activity across firms and national borders, in and of itself, has far-reaching consequences for economic growth and development. With this recognition I began to gravitate toward what had seemed like the minutiae of economic activity – the structure of firms, the precise characteristics of productive assets – and uncovered even more engaging questions about the causes and consequences of international economic integration.

I am deeply indebted to the many people and institutions whose support made this research possible. Perhaps my largest debt is to my dissertation advisor Jeff Frieden. My doctoral dissertation was the earliest incarnation of this book. Among many other things, Jeff taught me how to think systematically, especially while navigating uncharted intellectual territory. When I grew frustrated, he never failed to remind me "if it were easy someone would have done it already." These gifts of creativity and tenacity are priceless, and I am enormously grateful to Jeff for sharing them with me.

The other members of my dissertation committee offered thoughtful guidance throughout. Bob Bates shared his extensive knowledge of early FDI research and encouraged me to think about the consequences of my findings for economic development. Mike Hiscox helped me apply insights from trade policy to the study of FDI and convinced me to undertake the large data collection effort necessary to do this research. Torben Iversen introduced me to the idea that the organization of economic activity is of both political and economic consequence and helped me think about what that meant for the politics of FDI.

I had the great fortune to join the faculty of the University of Virginia at the same time David Leblang did. Every assistant professor should be so lucky to have a senior colleague like him. David is unfailingly generous with his time, advice, and enthusiasm. He read and commented on an early iteration of this book's manuscript and read many sections of subsequent drafts. As collaborators on subsequent projects, we have worked together to implement some of the ideas initially inspired by this book. I especially appreciate David's willingness to entertain some of my zanier research ideas that reach far into distant disciplines.

Over the many years I have worked on this research, several people have provided thoughtful feedback and suggestions: Jim Alt, Patrick Hanberry, James Harrigan, Nate Jensen, Mike Kellermann, Quan Li, Carol Mershon, Sachin Pandya, Pablo Pinto, Ken Scheve, Beth Simmons, and Robert Urbatch. Xun Cao and Jim Vreeland generously shared their data with me. Kishore Gawande, John Echeverri-Gent, Jeff Legro, David Leblang, and Lisa Martin read an early draft of the full manuscript and generously spent an entire day discussing it with me. Two anonymous reviewers for Cambridge University Press provided numerous suggestions that markedly improved the final product.

Several colleagues, past and present, provided support and encouragement in innumerable ways: Randy Akee, Ben Ansell, Dorothe Bach, Mark Copelovitch, Alison Criss, Asif Efrat, Tobias Hoffmann, SeoYoon Kim, Nathan Paxton, Sandra Sequiera, Catherine Thomas, Robert Urbatch, Alex Wagner, Gay Wehrli, and Joanna Lee Williams. David Andrew Singer has always been a particularly ready source of advice.

I am tremendously grateful to the several institutions and organizations that facilitated this research. Harvard's Weatherhead Center for International Affairs provided me with a warm and congenial environment when I was a graduate student. The Weatherhead Center also provided financial support, as did Harvard's Institute for Quantitative Social Science and Center for European Studies. In the year following graduate school, Princeton's Niehaus Center for Globalization and Governance, and its director Helen Milner, gave me the precious gifts of time and a vibrant community of like-minded scholars that eased the transition from graduate student to assistant professor. The University of Virginia's Bankard Fund for Political Economy generously supported the final stages of this research. Scott Parris, my editor at Cambridge University Press, provided sage advice throughout the publication process. His assistant, Kristin Purdy, was unfailingly helpful and ensured that the production process went smoothly.

My friends and family made this all possible in more ways than I can even begin to describe: Barbara de Lara Aguilar, Julian Blake, Peter Bruland, Arthi Chakravarthy, Katie Furman, Patrick Hanberry, Minona Heaviland, Shenandoah Joe, Anya Kapoor, Rahul Kapoor, Sachin Pandya, Sophia Pandya, Jessica Sager, Sheetal Sekhri, Kartini Shastry, Vidya Sundaram, and Jennifer Tromberg. I extend extra special thanks to my father Sharad Pandya for a lifetime of love, support, and encouragement to be aware of and curious about the world around me.

1

Introduction

The Politics of FDI Regulation in the Twentieth Century

Foreign direct investment (FDI) are investments that corporations make to produce goods and services in foreign countries. For example, these are the investments that a manufacturing firm makes when it relocates factories abroad, an oil company makes to drill for oil overseas, or a bank makes when it purchases a bank based in a foreign country.

FDI is the lynchpin of today's global economy, because it is the single largest form of international capital flow. In many years, the total value of world FDI flows exceeds the total value of all other forms of cross-border capital flows combined (UNCTAD 2012). Multinational corporations (MNCs) also create a significant portion of global trade. In the 1990s, MNCs generated 90 percent of all U.S. trade (Bernard, Jensen, and Schott 2009: 536). Intrafirm trade – trade between subsidiaries of the same MNC – accounts for more than a third of total world trade (Yi 2003, Bernard, Jensen, Redding, and Schott 2012).

FDI also figures prominently in some of the most pressing challenges and opportunities that global economic integration presents. FDI is unparalleled in its potential to foster economic development. When MNCs produce abroad, they provide a conduit for the specialized technologies and skills that are critical to industrialization (Romer 1993). During economic crises, including the 2008 global financial crisis, MNCs tend to increase stability, expanding production while their local counterparts fold (Desai, Foley, and Forbes 2008, Alfaro and Chen 2012).

There are, however, prominent examples of MNCs that appear to have run roughshod over national laws, and even basic human rights, to pursue resources and profits. A 1984 gas leak at a Union Carbide plant in Bhopal, India, left thousands of people dead and hundreds of thousands injured. Decades later, litigation over Union Carbide's negligence continued in both

Indian and U.S. courts. In 2012, the U.S. Supreme Court heard the case of twelve Nigerian citizens who alleged that the multinational oil company Royal Dutch Petroleum aided and abetted torture and extrajudicial killings by the Nigerian government. It eventually ruled in favor of Royal Dutch Petroleum.[1] Although these are extreme examples, they represent a larger class of concerns about how MNCs use their vast resources and influence, and how national laws cannot adequately hold MNCs accountable for their actions.

Political economy research on FDI has long focused on how politics influences patterns of FDI inflows across countries. Put differently, existing research emphasizes questions of FDI supply: How does politics factor into MNCs' location decisions? How do domestic political characteristics systematically influence the expected profits of FDI in a given host country? When investors own firms in foreign countries, they contend with political risk, the risk that host governments will change regulations, enforce contracts poorly, expropriate assets, or otherwise act to lower investment returns. Examining the politics of FDI from the perspective of MNCs, current FDI scholarship seeks to identify the host country characteristics that correspond to higher risks (Jensen et al. 2012). This research generally treats FDI as something of a black box, giving little regard to the specifics of MNCs' production and sales activities in host countries. Similarly, empirical analyses almost uniformly characterize FDI only by estimates of its monetary value.

In this book, I analyze how and why countries regulate FDI inflows. By contrast to existing research, my focus is on the politics of FDI demand: Why do countries restrict FDI inflows? Why are FDI restrictions more common in certain industries? Under what circumstances do countries dismantle regulations to provide MNCs greater access to their economy? These questions come from the perspective of citizens and national policy makers in host countries, not the investing MNCs. To answer these questions, I open up the black box of FDI to examine MNCs' specific economic activities and how those activities affect host countries.

FDI's economic consequences derive from the firm-specific economic assets that MNCs introduce into the countries in which they invest. These assets include production technologies, production practices, and consumer brands that the firm itself develops. MNCs engage in FDI to expand their production and sales into foreign markets while maintaining control over these assets. Firms for whom it is profitable to become multinational

---

[1]   Kiobel v. Royal Dutch Petroleum Co., 133 S.Ct. 1659 2013.

through FDI are firms whose assets confer exceptional productivity advantages. Indeed, MNCs are typically the world's most productive firms in their respective industries.

My theory of FDI regulation identifies how MNCs' production and sales activities redistribute income within host countries by increasing labor demand, and competing with local firms. National policy makers regulate FDI inflows to mitigate the expected costs to local firms. The most prevalent form of FDI regulation requires MNCs to form partnerships with local firms in which the local partner is the majority shareholder. These ownership restrictions facilitate local firms' access to MNCs' highly productive economic assets and the income they generate.

To test my claims, I use an original dataset of annual country-industry foreign ownership regulations that spans more than 100 countries during the 1970–2000 period. While there are multiple types of FDI policy instruments, ownership restrictions are the most ubiquitous form of FDI regulation across countries and industries. To the best of my knowledge, this is the most comprehensive dataset of formal national FDI regulations ever collected. With this data, I show why countries vary in how often they regulate FDI during the last third of the twentieth century.

This research contributes to our understanding of FDI policies and the politics of international economic integration more generally. For FDI specifically, it highlights the political underpinnings of the dramatic FDI liberalization during the 1970–2000 period, the liberalization responsible for FDI's prominent and varied role in economic integration today. Further, by identifying politically salient variation in the content of investments, this research resolves an apparent contradiction in the politics of FDI: the presence of both vociferous opposition to FDI and extensive efforts to attract FDI inflows. In addition to providing a theory of FDI demand, my research suggests new and better tests of political risk theories. These tests that emphasize variation across MNCs in their vulnerability and sensitivity to risk as much as they do variation in host-country sources of risk.

This research also situates the political economy of FDI in the context of larger structural transformations of the world economy. FDI liberalization is a microcosm of fundamental shifts in both the scope of political representation within countries and the global organization of economic activity that took place during the last third of the twentieth century. Democratization, and the accompanying expansion of political representation, prompted policy makers to reassess their countries' engagement in the global economy. Simultaneously, the emergence of multi-country production networks altered the costs and benefits of economic integration.

The book also provides insights into the unfolding politics of FDI in the twenty-first century. FDI features prominently in the relationship between advanced industrialized economies and large emerging-markets like China, India, and Brazil. FDI contributes heavily to the remarkable growth of these developing countries, particularly China. Investments to produce goods for export draw these countries into global production networks in which individual MNCs fragment their production of a single good across multiple countries. Through these networks developing countries gain high-quality manufacturing jobs and augment their industrial capacities.

FDI, however, also generates some of the sharpest economic policy tensions between advanced and emerging economies. While emerging-market countries welcome FDI that produces goods for export, they frequently restrict foreign MNCs' access to the local consumer market. Robust growth in these large countries makes them attractive destinations for MNCs seeking to produce and sell goods and services to their citizens. In response, emerging markets often reaffirm foreign ownership restrictions in non-traded service industries like retailing, finance, and telecommunications where MNCs pose a particularly large and direct competitive threat to local firms in the same industries. At the same time, MNCs based in emerging markets face increasing hostility toward their FDI into advanced economies. As developing countries' economies rapidly ascend, some of their largest firms have become MNCs, albeit frequently with subsidies from their national governments. In response to these investments, the world's most advanced economies are reassessing their policies, citing both economic and national security concerns, despite, in many cases, their having long been open to FDI.

These trends suggest that FDI remains as politically contentious as ever notwithstanding the decline in average levels of formal restrictions in recent decades. To understand today's global economy, we need to understand FDI's winners and losers and the evolution of FDI policies. In the concluding chapter, I return to the question of FDI's politics in the twenty-first century to discuss how this book's findings illuminate current and likely future controversies about FDI's roles in the global economy.

1.1 The Politicization of FDI Inflows: A Brief History

FDI is an artifact of modern industrial production, and in particular the central role of intellectual property that emerged in the early twentieth century (Chandler 1962). At the close the nineteenth century, FDI comprised an estimated 10 percent of global capital flows and was concentrated in infrastructure and natural resource extraction.[2] These investments flowed from major western European economies to their colonies and independent countries in the Americas (Teichova, Lévy-Leboyer, and Nussbaum 1986). Countries imposed few limits on FDI inflows. If anything, there were concerns in FDI source countries about dwindling investment capital for the domestic market.[3]

In the early twentieth century, private firms invested more heavily to create intellectual property through research, development, and marketing. Between 1921 and 1946, scientific personnel as a share of U.S. industrial employment increased sevenfold, because manufacturing firms established internal capacities for research and development (Frieden 2006: 165). These assets are firm-specific inasmuch as firms develop the assets for their exclusive use. The growing market for consumer products also raised returns on investments in product advertising. During the interwar period, European consumer products firms marketed directly to U.S. consumers. Switzerland's Nestle sold chocolate, and Britain's Lever Brothers Company became the leading soap manufacturer in the United States (Jones 2005).

FDI for the production of goods and services grew more popular during this period, because it allowed firms to exploit the scale economies that their intellectual property assets create. Firms can deploy these assets in multiple markets simultaneously, because they are intangible, allowing them to recoup more readily the initial fixed costs of creating the asset. As Chapter 2 explains in detail, firms choose FDI over alternative routes for capturing scale economies, like technology licensing, because in FDI firms retain control over their most valuable assets.

Firms organize their multinational production that uses these assets in one of two ways. Beginning in the interwar period, most MNCs organized their multinational production by replicating production and sales activities in multiple countries. This allowed them to circumvent the rising trade

[2] Svedberg (1978) argues that this common figure is an underestimate because it is inferred from public stock offerings (countries did not systematically collect and report data on capital flows in this era). By his calculations, FDI accounted for a large portion of capital flows into specific economies, including up to 50% of total capital inflows for countries/colonies in Asia, Africa, and Latin America. In many respects royally chartered trading companies such as the British East India Company were predecessors of the modern MNC.

[3] In the United States, specific FDI projects were occasionally controversial but there was little formal regulation. The federal government and several states passed laws barring foreigners from purchasing land and owning banks. A handful of additional regulations discriminated against foreign-owned firms. For instance, a 1791 federal law charged foreign ships higher customs duties and an 1817 law closed coastal trade routes to foreign merchants (Wilkins 1989).

barriers in this era and to compete for foreign customers in non-traded industries. In the decades following World War II, a growing number of MNCs pursued FDI to forge a global production networks that fragment production of a single product across multiple countries. By organizing production in this manner MNCs take advantage of lower production costs in foreign countries and export their output out of the host country. Global production networks became more efficient as transportation costs and host country trade barriers declined.

The iconic American toy, the Barbie doll, vividly illustrates this larger phenomenon of globalized production.[4] Barbie's "Made in China" label belies the toy's multinational origins. In 1996, the southern California-based Mattel Corporation sold "My First Tea Party Barbie" in the United States at a retail price of $9.99 per doll. Of this, $7.99 went directly to Mattel as profit and to defray the costs of domestic distribution and marketing. Sixty-five cents was paid for the raw materials and their processing: Saudi Arabian ethylene, a by-product of oil refining, and Taiwanese refining to convert the Saudi ethylene into the plastic pellets used in manufacturing the doll's body; Chinese cloth for the doll's clothing; nylon doll hair from Japan; and American machinery, molds, and paints. Thirty-five cents contributed to the wages of the 11,000 workers who assembled these components in two factories in Guangdong, China. The remaining $1 of the doll's purchase price went toward the transport of production inputs and finished dolls between the raw materials source countries, the Guangdong factories, and the United States, the doll's ultimate consumer market. Hong Kong acted as the hub of the production network. Inputs and final products were transported over land between Hong Kong and Guangdong and by sea between Hong Kong and all points abroad.

FDI first became politicized during the interwar period. Controversy centered on the perceived national security costs to the foreign ownership of productive assets, but limits on foreign ownership simultaneously advanced the interests of local producers vis-à-vis foreign MNCs. For example, when during World War I the U.S. government seized all enemy combatants' assets, among them were some 6,000 chemicals and pharmaceuticals patents owned by U.S. subsidiaries of German companies. At the time Germany was the world's leading producer of industrial chemicals and pharmaceuticals. While the United States justified the seizure on national security grounds, it also proved lucrative for U.S. chemicals producers. The federal government licensed the German patents to U.S. companies at

---

[4] "Barbie in the World Economy," *Los Angeles Times*, September 22, 1996.

minimal costs, and the previously lagging U.S. chemicals industry flourished (Wilkins 2004). These countries' situations were reversed after World War II when Western European countries voiced concerns about the dominance of U.S. corporations over the Continent's industrial production. The noted French intellectual Jean-Jacques Servan-Schreiber articulated these anxieties in his 1967 Europe-wide bestseller, *The American Challenge*:

The Common Market has become a New Far West for American businessmen. Their investments do not so much involve a transfer of capital, as an actual seizure of power within the European economy. Statistics fail to reflect the real gravity of the problem. … [T]he Common Market has become the New Frontier of American industry, its promised land. … If Europe continues to lag behind in electronics she could cease to be included among the advanced areas of civilization within a single generation. (Servan-Schreiber 1967: 11–14)

These examples demonstrate that even though politicians frame FDI inflows as a threat to national security or other vital national interests, there are also unmistakable distributive consequences to foreign ownership. U.S. subsidiaries of German chemicals companies dominated their American counterparts, but policy interventions transferred channeled German comparative advantage to U.S. firms. To be sure, there are genuine national interest reasons to regulate FDI, but to end the discussion at that would be to overlook these policies' clear distributive consequences.

My analysis of FDI regulation begins in the 1970s, the era of wide-scale adoption of foreign ownership restrictions as elements of broader industrialization strategies.[5] Although national security justifications first appeared following World War I, more explicitly economic motives for FDI restrictions first emerged following World War II. Decolonization in Asia and Africa produced an influx of new independent countries in the global economy. These countries, whose economies were previously centered around agriculture and mining, adopted comprehensive industrialization strategies

---

[5] A few industrialized countries including Japan, Australia, and Canada also frequently restricted FDI inflows (Chang 2003). The prevalence of state-owned enterprises and public ownership shares in private corporations have also been de facto barriers to investment. By law, foreign firms could not invest in sectors designated as public monopolies. MNCs often found it difficult to acquire ownership interests in firms with public participation because public shareholders could block such efforts. In Germany, tight connections between banks and industry made it difficult for MNCs to acquire local firms and to obtain local financing for investments. There is also anecdotal evidence of European countries pressuring MNCs to adopt production practices that facilitated technology transfer. For example, the United Kingdom allegedly pressured UK affiliates of Japanese electronics and automobile firms to source their inputs locally, restrict output, and export output rather than sell it domestically (Young et al. 1988).

to foster economic development. FDI regulations were a component of these strategies. Foreign ownership restrictions were designed to capture MNCs' production assets and a share of the revenue they generate for the gain of fledging local producers.

Ownership restrictions required MNCs to form partnerships with local firms, and policies like local content requirements forced MNCs to cultivate supplier relationships with local firms rather importing their production inputs. Many developing countries, particularly those in Latin America and Asia, restricted FDI most extensively. Although countries varied in their precise industrialization strategies, whether focused on producing goods for export or for local consumption in place of imports, FDI regulations served the same purpose: to secure access to production technologies necessary for industrialization that were otherwise unavailable (Haggard 1990). Many of these countries employed "complementary" policies designed to attract investments despite regulations, including weakening labor rights to keep MNCs' production costs artificially low. The next section describes these regulations in detail, as well as the transformation countries underwent toward greater FDI openness.

1.2 FDI Liberalization: Identifying Empirical Puzzles

By the end of the twentieth century, countries were considerably more open to FDI than they had been in the preceding decades. This transformation is evident on several dimensions. Figure 1.1 illustrates global trends in foreign ownership regulations and investment volumes.[6] In the mid-1970s, on average, countries protected nearly 35 percent of their industries by restricting foreign-owned firms to minority ownership (e.g., less than 50 percent equity). These regulations required MNCs to form partnerships with local firms to ensure that managerial control remained in local hands. Nearly three decades later, this figure had dropped to 10 percent.

MNCs also faced less hostile governments after making their investments. In 1975, there were more than eighty acts of expropriation against MNCs across nearly thirty countries.[7] Expropriations are host government actions that reallocate income generated by the MNCs' investment to domestic groups, such as ex post tax increases and the outright seizure of

---

[6] This figure plots the annual worldwide mean of *Entry Restriction*, an original measure of foreign ownership restriction. Chapter 3 and the Appendix provide extensive details on the sources and construction of the variable.

[7] Jodice (1980: 181). See also Kobrin (1980) and Minor (1994) for a detailed discussion of expropriation trends.

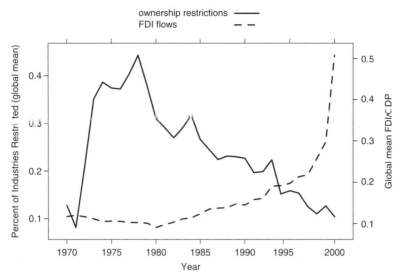

Figure 1.1 Global average foreign-ownership restrictions and FDI stock, 1970–2000.
Note: Foreign-ownership restrictions data are as described in text. Global FDI stock data are from Lane and Milesi-Ferretti (2007).

MNCs' property. A decade later, these acts were not only exceedingly rare, but many countries revised national investment laws to explicitly guarantee the property rights of foreign-owned firms.

Greater FDI openness is evident in international economic cooperation as well. In 1974, developing countries advanced the New International Economic Order, a set of UN resolutions intended to recast international economic rules in their favor. Among other things, those countries demanded an internationally recognized right to regulate MNCs' activities in their countries, and a right to expropriate foreign investments in order to secure a greater portion of the income they generate. These demands reflected a widely shared sentiment during this era that MNCs not only exploited developing countries but also reinforced global wealth inequality. By contrast, in the World Trade Organization's (WTO) Uruguay Round of global trade talks completed in 1994, most of these same countries signed the Treaty on Trade-Related Investment Measures to eliminate laws that required MNCs, operating in their countries, to source their production inputs locally. Many WTO members also formally pledged to provide MNCs with greater access to service industries like telecommunications and banking. A growing number of preferential trade agreements also stipulate openness to FDI from multinational firms based in other signatory countries.

Not only did countries dismantle policy barriers to FDI, but they also more actively courted MNCs. Between 1990 and 1995, the number of new bilateral investment treaties nearly quadrupled after three decades of minimal treaty activity (Elkins, Guzman, and Simmons 2006). These treaties codify extensive guarantees of MNCs' property rights to address firms' concerns about expropriation. Some of these treaties even grant foreign MNCs legal standing in domestic courts – an unprecedented right in international law. A growing number of countries directly subsidize MNCs' investments through tax incentives, land grants, discounted production inputs, and other de facto transfers (Oman 2000). For example, in 1996, Daimler-Benz established a manufacturing plant in the Brazilian state of Minas Gerais to produce Mercedes automobiles. National and state governments furnished tax breaks and financial incentives to the tune of $340,000 for each job that the plant directly created (Oman 2000: 32). In the 1980s, the state of Kentucky attracted a Toyota Motor Corporation assembly plant with a combination of land grants from the state, $47 million in new road construction to meet the plant's transportation needs, and a further $65 million of public funds for employee training programs (Graham and Krugman 1995: 89). Many countries streamline regulations so as to regulate foreign firms less than native firms. All of these measures are designed to attract FDI with the expectation that their investments will foster economic growth and development by creating high-skilled jobs and introducing productivity-boosting technologies.

Within this general trend of FDI liberalization, there are distinct patterns of variation in frequency of regulation across countries and industries. These patterns reveal country and industry characteristics that influence FDI policy making. Temporal changes in these country and industry characteristics help pinpoint explanations for why countries liberalize their foreign investment regimes.

The clearest trend across countries is that developing countries impose higher average ownership restrictions than do industrialized countries. Figure 1.2 plots the same measure of average foreign ownership restrictions as in Figure 1.1 but disaggregated into two groups: the advanced industrialized countries that belong to the Organization for Economic Cooperation and Development (OECD), and non-OECD countries, a proxy for low- and middle-income countries. The figure reveals that non-OECD countries account for most FDI restrictions historically and continue to regulate at higher average levels than the most advanced countries. At the height of restrictions in the mid-1970s, the average non-OECD country restricted ownership in half of all industries in its economy. By comparison, the average OECD country rarely restricted more than 10 percent of industries.

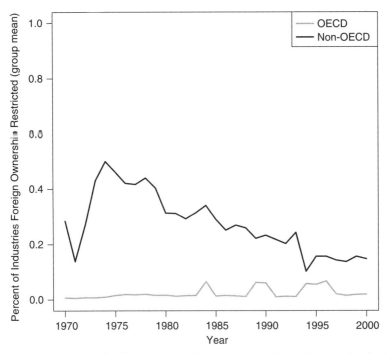

Figure 1.2 Average level of foreign ownership restriction, advanced versus developing countries.

Note: Foreign-ownership restrictions are measured with the *Entry Restrictions* (variable as described in the text). OECD countries in sample: Australia (since 1971), Austria, Belgium, Canada, Denmark, Finland, France, Germany, Greece, Iceland, Ireland, Italy, Japan, Mexico (since 1994), Luxembourg, Netherlands, New Zealand (since 1973), Portugal, South Korea (since 1996), Spain, Sweden, Switzerland, Turkey, and the United Kingdom. See Appendix for all countries classified as non-OECD members.

Average restrictions also vary by region. Figure 1.3 plots average restrictions over the 1970–2000 period by geographic region. Asia and Latin America stand out for the most dramatic fluctuations over the sample period. These countries appear to drive much of the variation in regulations over time. Overall levels are low in Western Europe/Canada and Africa, albeit with a slight upward trend in the latter case. Middle East/North Africa countries have liberalized somewhat, but overall levels remained the world's highest in 2000. One puzzle, then, is why countries vary in their propensity to deploy FDI restrictions such that less-developed countries, particularly those in Latin America and Asia, used them more frequently in the 1970s but dismantled them over the following three decades.

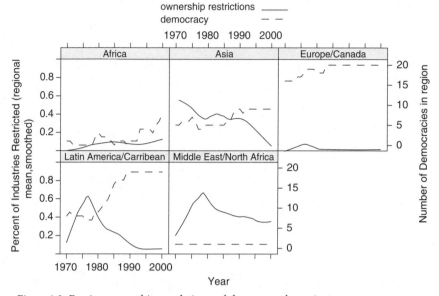

Figure 1.3 Foreign ownership regulation and democracy, by region.
Note: This figure plots the annual global mean of *Entry Restriction* and number of democracies worldwide (*Democracy* = 1). See Appendix for region classifications.

FDI regulations also vary systematically across industries. Countries subjected some industries to ownership restrictions more frequently than others. Table 1.1 summarizes the number of countries that imposed foreign ownership regulations across several manufacturing and services industries in 1978 and 2000.[8] At both points in time, there were more countries that limited foreign ownership in service industries than in manufacturing industries. Over time, most industries saw the number of countries with regulations decline, but more countries liberalized ownership in manufacturing industries than in service industries. By 2000, on average seven fewer countries restricted ownership in manufacturing industries as compared to 1978. For service industries, only about three fewer countries eliminated ownership limits.

To explain these multiple patterns in the frequency of FDI regulations, we need political economy theories of FDI regulation that can explain what is distinctive about FDI across these dimensions. The following section provides such a theory.

---

[8] These data are the *Restrictions Counts* variable that I analyze in Chapter 6.

Table 1.1 *Frequency of industry-level foreign-ownership restrictions, 1978 versus 2000*

	N countries with restrictions	
	1978	2000
Manufacturing		
Chemicals	13	6
Communications & audio and visual equipment	13	6
Computers	13	6
Fabricated metal products	13	6
Food	13	6
Glass and non-metallic mineral products	14	6
Instruments and related products	13	6
Motor vehicles, bodies and trailers, and parts	13	6
Non-motor vehicle transport equipment	13	6
Paper products	14	6
Printing & publishing industries	13	6
Textiles, apparel, and leather products	13	6
Wood products	14	6
Services		
Finance except depository institutions & securities	22	15
Insurance carriers and related activities	20	23
Public utilities	19	14.5
Real estate services	13	17
Retail trade	19	13
Telecommunications	19	15
Transportation	18.25	14

Note: Foreign ownership restrictions data aggregated from International Standard Industrial Classification (ISIC) to industry classifications from the US Bureau of Economic Analysis (BEA) 1977 and 1999 Benchmark Surveys. Industries listed are those present in both surveys. Exceptions: 1977 survey combined Telecommunications and Public utilities into a single category so the same value is entered for both industries. Computers 1977 value is for Office machines; Communications equipment 1977 is Radio, television, and communications equipment. The 1999 value for Communications equipment is for nonaffiliate sales because distribution of sales data could not be computed due to data suppressed for privacy reasons. Fractional values in Public utilities and Transport are due to averaging across multiple categories (public utilities = ISIC industries 40,41, transport = ISIC industries 60–63).

1.3 The Political Economy of FDI Regulation: Theoretical Claims and Empirical Tests

My theory of FDI regulation describes the winners and losers from FDI inflows and politicians' incentives to privilege the interests of either side. The economic consequences of MNCs' activities drive citizens' preferences for FDI regulation. These firms undertake FDI to produce, and sometimes sell, goods and services in a foreign country. Divisions over the desirability of FDI inflows emerge because multinational firms' production raises labor demand and their sales activities heighten market competition. Labor embraces FDI in anticipation of higher wages, whereas local firms, facing higher labor costs and stiffer sales competition, prefer limits.

Politicians regulate FDI to advance the interests of the more politically influential faction. In democracies politicians are accountable to the broad electorate, whereas in autocracies politicians are beholden to a narrow subset of the population to maintain their position. All else being equal, democracies have lower average FDI restrictions because the expected wages increases accrue to labor, a broader subset of the electorate. In autocracies, by contrast, politicians tend to restrict FDI inflows in line with local firms' preferences.

The theory explains why countries generally liberalized FDI inflows and highlights why patterns of FDI regulation vary over time across both countries and industries. Historically autocratic developing countries regulated FDI more extensively than democracies – consistent with my theory of politicians' incentives. Democratization in these countries over the period 1970–2000 produced FDI liberalization, reflecting the shifting incentives of national policymakers.

The emergence of democracy, the so-called Third Wave of democracy that began in the late 1970s and proceeded through the end of the century, was one of the most transformative political developments of the late twentieth century (Huntington 1991). These newly democratized countries were concentrated among the developing nations of Latin America and Asia. Democratization produced lower regulations on FDI because it elevated labor's policy preferences in the policy-making process. Prior to democratization, most developing countries adhered to some form of state-led industrialization strategy. Although these strategies varied, they rested upon a similar political foundation of labor repression and disproportionate political influence for a small, nascent industrial class.

The political status of labor links FDI's distributive effects to policy outcomes through labor's political voice. In political systems that devise some form of politician accountability to the electorate, the act of voting provides politicians incentives to heed voters' preferences. Labor can participate in the political process in a more organized fashion through rights to organize into unions and through the representation of labor interests. These vehicles for collective political participation provide additional conduits for labor's preferences to enter the political process. These groups can lobby for preferred policies, to inform their constituencies, and in the case of political parties, to advance labor's interests in formal policy-making institutions. Analogous to my proposed mechanism, existing studies confirm that democratization contributes to trade and portfolio capital liberalization (Quinn and Inclan 1997, Eichengreen and Leblang 2008, Milner and Mukherjee 2009). Following democratization in many countries labor enjoyed relatively more political clout through the expansion of voting rights, unfettered labor organizations, and the emergence of left-leaning parties. With greater labor participation in policy making, there were stronger incentives to remove distortions and to attract the forms of FDI that generate jobs and bring with them more dynamic technologies.

Opposition to FDI is more intense in industries in which multinational firms both produce and sell in the local market rather than produce for export. In the former type of industry, local firms contend with higher labor costs and more competition, whereas export-oriented FDI only raises labor costs. The growth of export-oriented FDI accounts for greater openness in manufacturing industries and the persistence of regulations in local market-oriented service industries. Export-oriented FDI began in earnest in the 1990s as more countries committed to opening their economies to free trade through the use of free trade agreements. With countries' commitments to free trade firmly entrenched, MNCs more actively rearranged their production to leverage the distinctive production advantages of other countries. This occurred as part of a larger move to fragment production across borders in the pursuit of lower production costs.

To explain why countries regulate FDI inflows, one has to make sense of observable policy variation across countries and industries. To accomplish this, the explanation has to link country and industry attributes to the preference for regulation and/or the process by which countries set regulations. Additionally, it has to map changes in those country and industry characteristics over time to temporal patterns in regulations. Chapters 2 and 3 provide a unified theoretical foundation from which I derive testable claims about the country and industry variation in the frequency of FDI limits.

Nuanced theoretical claims require equally nuanced data to assess their validity. One of this book's central contributions is the variety of data, much of it original, featured in its empirical tests. I confirm that individual preferences for FDI are consistent with my hypothesized distributive effects by analyzing public opinion data for seventeen Latin American countries. These microlevel tests account for a variety of other economic and noneconomic factors that could influence individual support for FDI.

My tests of cross-national and cross-industry variation in foreign-ownership restrictions are based on measures of formal regulations generated from an original comprehensive dataset of ownership regulation collected as part of this research. First and foremost, these data allow for direct tests of formal regulations. Each set of analyses considers a wide range of alternate explanations. Tests of cross-country variation include controls for economic crises and external influences on the level of FDI regulation. Analyses of industry-level variation incorporate industry characteristics that mediate FDI's distributive effects or industries' collective action costs.

1.4 New Perspectives on the Political Economy of FDI

At the beginning of this chapter, I contrasted my focus on countries' demand for FDI with existing research's focus on MNCs' willingness to supply FDI. The lack of research on FDI regulation and other aspects of FDI demand is puzzling. Among the most fundamental questions that international political economy scholars consider is the relative demand for economic openness within countries. In answering this question, policy outcomes – tariff rates, capital controls, immigrant quotas, and accession to international economic agreements – are typically of primary interest, because these policies directly reflect the relative demand for openness. In this section, I elaborate on the FDI demand/supply distinction to underscore this book's theoretical and empirical innovations to political economy research.

There are two distinct generations of FDI research, one on either end of the time period that I analyze, 1970–2000. In both waves, scholars tightly focused their research on the prevailing politics of FDI at that time. Among the first generation of FDI scholars were those inspired by dependency theories of (under)development. They posited that FDI policies reflected a fundamental alliance among host-country policy makers and foreign and local capital owners to suppress labor in developing countries (Evans 1979). Another group of early FDI scholars argued that MNCs and host countries had an inherently antagonistic relationship. Host countries sought to extract as much wealth and technology as possible from MNCs, while MNCs endeavored to protect themselves from host country predation (Vernon 1971, Kobrin 1987).

The second and current generation of research emerged in the 2000s, seemingly inspired by countries' vigorous efforts to attract FDI during this period. These scholars primarily departed from earlier research by identifying host-country political circumstances in which policymakers have incentives to maximize FDI inflows in their countries. Earlier theories did not envision scenarios in which policy makers had incentives for wide-scale FDI openness. Most second-generation research correlates the amount of

FDI that countries receive with specific host-country sources of relative political risk. These host-country characteristics include regime type and constraints on policy makers (Henisz 2000, Li and Resnick 2003, Jensen 2006), the scope of executive autonomy (Li 2009), government partisanship (Pinto and Pinto 2008), and participation in multilateral trade and investment agreements (Büthe and Milner 2008, Tobin and Busch 2010). As a whole, second-generation FDI research provides insights into the political characteristics that encourage policy makers to prey on MNCs.

While the evolution of FDI research broadly tracks substantive patterns in FDI openness, none of this research actually explains why, over time, countries grew more open to FDI. While current research emphasizes how MNCs respond to specific aspects of political representation and institutions, it usually does not directly analyze specific host government policies and actions vis-à-vis multinationals. Existing research leaves unresolved longstanding contradictions about the politics of FDI. If FDI has long been a source of new jobs and technology, why the previous hostility toward MNCs? By the same token, MNCs have long provoked controversies over the negative consequences of their investments within recipient countries. If so, why do restrictions in some industries persist despite overall liberalization?

My theory of FDI regulation resolves this apparent contradiction by identifying cross-industry sources of variation in FDI's distributive effects, cross-national sources of variation in policymakers' incentives to regulate FDI inflows, and changes over time along both dimensions. This theory provides several innovations relative to existing supply-side theories. With regard to FDI preferences, it shows why local capital strictly prefers FDI under conditions of foreign ownership regulations to unregulated FDI and why the intensity of that preference varies across industries.

Additionally, my research identifies new testable implications of existing supply-side theories. Supply and demand-side theories share the same underlying premise that policy makers see in FDI the potential to extract value from MNCs. My emphasis on ex ante regulation, as opposed to the existing research's emphasis on ex post takings, is a more precise outcome from which to draw inferences about the domestic politics of FDI. Supply-side theories infer the presence of political risk from correlations between institutional characteristics and changes in the total volume of FDI inflows. Even with the best quality data on FDI inflows, the outcome of changes in FDI flows is conceptually several steps removed from what is being modeled, MNCs' decisions, and the underlying concept of political risk is a broad category that includes everything from unexpected policy changes with adverse implications for profitability to direct expropriation of MNC assets.[9]

With the new data collected for this study, we now have a direct measure of the political demand for FDI, rather than a disparate set of factors that constitute an investment climate. These data address what is perhaps the biggest challenge to more detailed studies of FDI: the paucity of comprehensive and reliable data. Existing FDI research relies heavily on FDI estimates from national balance of payments data. Considerable measurement error aside (Beugelsdijk et al. 2010), these data reinforce the black box of FDI by reducing investment to its monetary value. The appendix to this book describes the range of policy instruments that countries use to limit FDI inflows and assesses the merits of existing proxies for FDI policies.

By focusing on specific FDI regulatory instruments, I also highlight that the political economy of FDI demand is not about whether FDI itself is desirable, but whether unrestricted FDI is preferable to restricted FDI. Existing empirical studies make few attempts to control for FDI regulation when modeling FDI volumes.[10] These models may incorrectly estimate the importance of political institutions by omitting the formal restrictions that emerge as a consequence of institutions.

1.5 Roadmap

The body of this book, Chapters 2–6, unfolds over two sections. This first section, Chapters 2 and 3, lays the theoretical foundations for my claims. Chapter 2 begins with the question why does FDI exist? It introduces the reader to FDI as a form of economic activity and to key concepts in industrial organization that explain what kinds of firms pursue FDI and how they organize their production across countries. Readers with substantial background in industrial organization and the mechanics of FDI may skim the first half of Chapter 2.

The second half of Chapter 2 outlines FDI's distributive effects and identifies testable implications for individual FDI preferences, cross-national variation in ownership restrictions, and cross-industry variation in ownership restrictions. From the host country perspective, FDI is the inflow of highly productive and industry specific capital. I use a standard specific

---

[9] Notable exceptions are models of expropriation counts (Li 2009) and tests of political risk's effects on firm behavior (Jensen 2008).

[10] For example, Li and Resnick (2003) and Jensen (2003) employ general measures of capital controls to control for ownership restrictions. I discuss the shortcomings of this proxy and existing alternatives in the Appendix.

factors trade model to derive FDI's effects on wages and returns to local firms. FDI drives a wedge between labor and capital by raising local labor demand and, when MNCs invest to compete in local product markets, by increasing product market competition. This configuration of preferences is the opposite of the familiar result from trade policy of labor-capital unity in the presence of specific factors. I discuss a number of distributive effects that are outside of the model's scope and describe how empirical tests in subsequent chapters confirm that they do not alter alignments. I outline three sets of hypotheses that follow from the model.

In Chapter 3, I turn to the question of why countries restrict FDI inflows. If firms' central motive is to maintain control over their productive assets, countries restrict FDI inflows to weaken this control by channeling the assets and their associated income streams to domestic capital owners. Ownership restrictions that limit MNCs to a minority equity share of any single company serve this purpose by requiring MNCs to form partnership with domestic firms. I estimate a model of FDI inflow volumes and find that countries that impose ownership restrictions on a larger proportion of their industries receive less investment.

I devote Chapters 4–6, to empirical tests of these three sets of claims. Chapter 4 provides an analysis of individual-level FDI preferences using Latin American survey data from the 1990s. I find that respondents' probability of supporting unrestricted FDI inflows corresponds to the expected effects of FDI on their income; the greater the expected rise, the more likely a respondent is to support FDI into their country. Additionally, I rule out several alternate explanations for FDI preferences including concerns about job security and privatization, and anti-foreigner sentiment. These findings validate the economic-distributive microfoundation of my theory.

In Chapter 5 I turn to the puzzle of cross-national variation in regulations such that developing countries, particularly Latin American and East Asian countries, exhibit high levels of ownership regulation that steadily decline between 1970 and 2000. I show that countries remove ownership restriction following democratization. This finding is robust to a variety of other documented catalysts for economic reform including economic crises, the dictates of multilateral creditors, and the diffusion through peer countries. I also confirm that countries do not replace formal regulations with less transparent but functionally equivalent FDI barriers. These findings establish empirically how changes in policy makers' incentives to regulate FDI inflows contributed to an overall liberalization of FDI.

Chapter 6 focuses on a third set of claims regarding cross-industry variation in the frequency with which countries restrict foreign ownership. FDI's distributive effects vary based on the activities that MNCs undertake in host countries. Where local firms must compete with MNCs for both workers and customers, those firms have greater incentives to lobby for ownership restrictions than local firms that face competition only for workers. I estimate a count model of the number of countries that restricted ownership into a given industry in 2000. Despite considerable liberalization in the preceding decades, there remained marked variation among the industries most frequently regulated. I show that industries into which higher proportions of total FDI are market-oriented investments face ownership restrictions in more countries. This finding reflects the growth of export-oriented FDI as a mode of organizing multinational production. The model includes controls for a variety of industry characteristics that may influence the magnitude of costs to local firms including product differentiation, the scope for positive technology spillovers, or the costs of collective action. The findings reported in this chapter highlight how fundamental shifts in global production facilitated greater FDI openness by relieving some of the burdens that FDI imposes on local firms.

Chapter 7 reviews the book's central findings and considers how they can be built upon. For political economy scholars, these findings suggest a new research program on the political economy of international production that combines both international trade and investment. I also show how this book's insights apply to current economic disputes between advanced economies and large emerging markets such as China and India. Although foreign ownership restrictions remain low, FDI remains as politically contentious as ever. Using the theory from Chapter 2, I unpack these disputes to reveal persistent underlying distributive conflicts over FDI. I conclude by identifying how these conflicts are likely to evolve with broader economic and political trends in the world economy.

2

FDI

Why Companies Invest and Countries Restrict

In 1849, Eberhard Farber moved to the United States to sell pencils. He was the youngest son in the family that owned A. W. Farber, Germany's leading lead-pencil manufacturer. Eberhard Farber was tasked with not only selling the company's goods in the United States but also identifying new sources of red cedar, the wood used to make pencils in the company's main factory near Nuremberg. Within a decade, Farber had become a U.S. citizen, built a lumber mill in Florida to process cedar wood for export back to Germany, and developed new manufacturing equipment and product lines for his company. Among his inventions during this period: the first pencil topped with an eraser.

In 1861, faced with growing U.S. demand for pencils amid steep import duties, Farber established the United States' first pencil factory on 42nd Street in Manhattan on the site occupied today by the United Nations headquarters. This factory expanded A.W. Farber's multinational holdings, which already included the company's main manufacturing facility and smaller operations in Bavaria (overseen by Farber's older brothers); subsidiaries in Paris and London; and a distributor in Vienna. Shortly after the New York factory began operations, a local newspaper described how Farber had adapted his family's pencil manufacturing process to the different production conditions he had encountered in the United States:

The cost of labor is so much higher in this country than in Europe, that machinery had to be devised and constructed to automatically perform the work, which is done so cheaply by hand in the old country. In fact, the whole process of necessary machinery was invented ... and Mr. Farber had the satisfaction of knowing that he could not only make pencils in this country cheaper, but also of a much better and more uniform finish than any produced before.[1]

[1] This quote and the preceding details are from Wilkins (1989, 132–133).

Farber's experience illustrates the range of FDI's effects in recipient countries. What began as a simple business to market imported pencils and to source raw lumber quickly expanded to include industrial infrastructure – a lumber mill and manufacturing plant, new global economic linkages through the export of cedar from the United States to Germany, and technological innovation in both consumer products and in manufacturing equipment. If A.W. Farber had simply imported wood from the United States and exported finished pencils from Germany, the company would have achieved its goal without the infrastructure costs and technological innovation that accompanied its direct investment in the United States. Why does a company like Farber, or any firm for that matter, choose FDI over less costly alternatives?

This chapter examines firms' motives to undertake FDI and the distributive consequences of FDI for recipient countries in order to derive testable claims about FDI preferences and policymaking. By delving into firms' motives for FDI, I identify the range of economic activities that can occur through these investments. In turn, an accurate account of FDI motives and content helps identify how FDI affects demand for factors of production and product prices in host countries.

To begin, consider the role of firm-specific assets in production and the productivity advantages that those assets create. An asset is any type of economic resource that produces value. An asset is specific to a single firm when, all else equal, only that firm can derive its full value.[2] Usually these are assets that the firm itself has developed. The firm is in the unique position to maximize the value of the asset, because of its superior knowledge of the asset and the asset's complementarities with the firm's other assets. Most firm-specific assets are intangible intellectual property, such as production technologies, product innovations, managerial and organizational practices, and trademarked brands. Firms develop these assets through internal research and development or marketing activities. Chapter 1 described how these types of assets have been the centerpiece of modern production since the early twentieth century.

Firms choose to become multinational to expand into foreign markets while maintaining control over their firm-specific assets. Alternative strategies may diminish the value of these assets. A. W. Farber, for example, could have licensed its pencil-making technology to an American firm rather than

---

[2] In practice, asset specificity is a continuum so there is variation in the extra value that the originating firm derives from the asset.

directly entering the market. Technology licensing would generate returns to the firm's specific assets by taking advantage of growing U.S. demand for pencils and bypassing import barriers. Such licensing agreements, however, leave firms vulnerable to the theft or degradation of their proprietary knowledge. Instead, firms expand across national borders to expand internationally while keeping assets within the firm

MNCs are those firms whose firm-specific assets confer exceptional productivity advantages. Firms that become multinational are not a representative sample of world firms. These are highly productive firms for whom FDI is profitable, despite the substantial costs involved in both establishing and operating foreign subsidiaries. The Farber case illustrates why firm-specific knowledge matters for generating the different forms of economic activity that MNCs undertake. None of the positive externalities in that example would have existed had Eberhard Farber not known as much as he did about pencil production when he arrived in the United States. Likewise, all firms that undertake FDI possess exclusive specialized assets that are the primary source of their competitive advantage.

Identifying the motives for FDI also help us model FDI's distributive effects, that is, explain the ways that FDI creates winners and losers in the countries that receive FDI. This model, in turn, implies testable claims about the sources of variation in FDI preferences and policies. Chapter 1 identified two specific puzzles about variation in FDI regulation. First, countries vary in how much they regulate FDI. Developing countries regulated foreign ownership more extensively relative to industrialized countries during the sample period 1970–2000. Countries in Latin America and East Asia exhibited particularly marked fluctuation relative to other regions. Second, FDI regulation varies by industry: Services industries are more often regulated than manufacturing industries and saw lower declines in regulation over the sample period. This trend is evident even at the end of the sample period when overall regulation levels were at their lowest.

The ways in which firms organize their investments across countries provides another analytical building block by indicating the range of activities that MNCs undertake in host countries. Some MNCs produce for export whereas others produce and sell within the local market. The organization of production is important to understanding why countries shift toward economic liberalization over time, because it links larger shifts in the world economy to the change in the content of FDI's distributive effects.

To derive FDI's distributive consequences in recipient countries, I apply the specific-factors model of international trade to FDI. Political economy scholars have long relied on this model to establish the economic costs and benefits of economic integration (Mussa 1974, Neary 1978, Frieden 1991, Hiscox 2002), but this is its first application to FDI. The model is particularly suited to this purpose, because it assumes that capital is specific to the production of one good, and thereby captures the highly specific capital assets at stake in FDI. Assets are firm-specific in as much as their value is maximized when deployed in a single firm. However, these firms compete in industrywide product markets. The model consists of two industries and labor that is mobile across industries.[3]

The specific factors model is also well suited to assessing FDI's distributive effects because it treats capital as immobile across industries within an economy. Within this context, FDI inflows increase the supply of productive capital in one industry. The model delivers clear implications for how this increase in firm/industry-specific capital changes the income of existing firms and labor, revealing a stark division between labor and capital. Local labor enjoys wage increases, making it a natural supporter of unrestricted FDI inflows. Local firms oppose FDI inflows, because they raise labor costs and, in some cases, introduce product market competition. This prediction is the exact opposite of the model's predictions regarding trade policy. In the case of FDI factor specificity drives a wedge between capital and labor rather than uniting them.

The first half of this chapter explains why firms would choose to become multinational and which firms actually have. These fundamentals of FDI are necessary to precisely specify what economic activities MNCs engage in and how they compare to local firms in the countries in which they invest. The second half of the chapter derives testable hypotheses from a model of FDI's distributive effects. The first section applies the specific factors model to derive the effect of FDI inflows for factor incomes in recipient countries. It also identifies several important features of FDI that fall outside of the model's scope to establish the robustness tests necessary to verify the predictions of the basic model. Each of the following three sections builds on the model's implication to develop testable claims about the sources of FDI preferences, cross-national, and cross-industry variation in foreign

[3] As I discuss, my claims regarding FDI's implications for labor do not depend on cross-industry labor mobility. On the contrary, my claim should be more likely to hold when labor is industry-specific because the returns on entry to industry-specific capital are greater than for mobile labor.

ownership regulations, respectively. This chapter's conclusion outlines the empirical tests of these claims in subsequent chapters.

2.1 Why Does FDI Exist?

2.1.1 FDI Protects Firm-Specific Assets

While firm-specific assets can take a variety of forms, they share two essential characteristics. First, these assets are intangible. Although there can be tangible manifestations of the assets, like machinery, much of these assets' value resides in the knowledge that went into their conception and creation rather than in any inherent worth. For example, pharmaceutical drugs or software programs derive their value mainly from the intellectual property that went into their creation rather than in the physical outputs of a pill or a computer disc. Second, firm-specific assets arise in bundles, such that the full value of any single asset is realized only when it is deployed in concert with other firm-specific assets, i.e., as part of a bundle. In the example of A. W. Farber's U.S. investments, the value of the firm's Florida cedar mill came from the firm's expertise in pencil production. Absent that knowledge, the mill would have been less valuable to the firm.

The intangible and bundled character of assets presents firms with two dilemmas in their pursuit of returns to the assets. First, for any single asset, firms have the choice of retaining the asset for their exclusive use, or licensing it for use to another firm. In the latter scenario, the asset-owning firm allows a separate firm use of its assets in exchange for a fee. For example, Yoplait is a brand of yogurt owned by a French company of the same name. The company licenses its brand name, an intangible, firm-specific asset, to the U.S. firm General Mills who produces and sells yogurt in the United States under the Yoplait brand name. Firms license assets when the cost of pursuing a market opportunity exceeds the expected return. Yoplait earns more in licensing fees than it would by selling yogurt itself in the United States, because the company's cost of producing and distributing yogurt exceeds the expected return to entering the U.S. market.

The downside of licensing is that firms are vulnerable to the theft or degradation of their asset. The intangibility of intellectual property makes it risky to engage in arms-length transactions, market-mediated transactions between separate entities. It is inherently difficult to construct a market for ideas. In order to provide potential buyers with sufficient information about assets, owners have to divulge some of the knowledge that constitutes the assets' value (Gatignon and Andersen 1988). As an added difficulty, after the transaction, the licensee has incentives to renege on the contract, having received much of the productive value of the asset upfront (Horstmann and Markusen 1987, Ethier and Markusen 1996). The firm that owns that asset loses not only licensing fees, but also its share of any future income that the licensee earns by using the asset. Even when the licensee honors the licensing agreement, there are other ways in which licensing can diminish asset value. For instance the licensee may produce poor quality goods under the originating firm's brand name, thus damaging the portion of the brand's value that derives from the brand's reputation for quality. Alternately, the licensee could profit from the originating firm's marketing efforts without contributing to their cost. Degradation lowers the future expected income from the asset.

Asset owners face this dilemma, because typically the parties in the transaction cannot ex-ante write a contract that will deter predation by one party against the other. This is a basic principal-agent problem. Parties to the agreement wish to maximize their income even if it is at the expense of the other party. The licensing firm can only monitor the licensee imperfectly. Some firms are willing to assume these risks or are able to design contracts to which all parties have incentives to adhere. Firms that cannot adequately minimize these risks of licensing prefer to retain control over their firm-specific intellectual property.

Firms' second dilemma concerns how much control to retain over the full bundle of assets that are inputs into a single product. Consider the production of automobiles. Automobile production requires assembling many discrete parts into a finished automobile. An automaker, like any other firm, has to choose which parts to make itself and which parts to buy from separate supplier firms. Relying on outside suppliers allows firms to specialize (Klein, Crawford, Alchian 1978, Williamson 1973). For example, a supplier of engine parts to an auto manufacturer would, in theory, find it more efficient to customize manufacturing equipment to the auto manufacturer's unique specifications. Likewise, the automaker could completely outsource production of parts to the supplier and redirect its production capacity elsewhere. Both firms become more efficient by specializing their production.

Specialization, however, creates risks for both the supplier and producer. Both firms need to make specialized investments based on their relationship. The parts supplier may customize its production equipment to the precise specifications of one automaker, but the value of this specialization is contingent on an ongoing relationship with that one automaker. Due to specialized output there are no other automakers to whom the supplier can sell parts. Similarly, an automaker may eliminate its capacity to produce a specific part, choosing to rely exclusively on an outside parts supplier. As a consequence the automaker cannot produce cars without the supplier's parts.

The primary risk in relationship-specific investments such as these is that they leave all sides vulnerable to holdup. Holdup occurs when one party to a contract threatens to end the relationship unless the terms of the contact are renegotiated (Monteverde and Teece 1982, Ethier 1986). The threatening party takes advantage of the other party's dependence to press for more favorable terms. For example, the parts supplier may refuse to provide parts to the automaker unless there is a pay increase. Likewise the automaker may threaten to stop buying the supplier's parts unless the supplier lowers its price. Holdup is the downside of relying on other firms for production inputs. For some firms the risks are great enough that they choose to produce their own inputs. Similar to the licensing scenario, firms sacrifice higher returns on their assets in order to retain control over their assets.

The risks of licensing and relationship-specific investments are magnified when the parties to a contract reside in different countries. When the parties to a contract, whether a licensing agreement or a supply agreement, are in the same country, they are subject to the same contract laws.[4] They can rely on domestic courts to adjudicate contract disputes. By contrast, an international context adds uncertainty about the legal jurisdiction in which any contract disputes would be resolved. Domestic courts can be biased in favor of the party from their jurisdiction, leaving aggrieved firms with little recourse. All else equal, international contracts are more risky than domestic contracts both for technology licensing and for supplier-producer relationships.

FDI exists, because of the high risks entailed in international technology-licensing contracts and in supplier-producer contracts.[5] FDI is the cross-border expansion of firms through the creation of foreign subsidiaries. A multinational corporation is a firm with subsidiaries in more than one country; many MNCs operate in multiple countries simultaneously. FDI overcomes the risks of international contracts by expanding the firm itself across international borders.[6] Through this expansion, FDI keeps firm-specific intellectual property within the firm. FDI eliminates the conflicting

---

[4] Nunn (2007) identifies the importance of contract enforcement to sustaining supplier-producer relationships of traded goods.

[5] Hymer (1976) was the first to define FDI in these terms.

[6] In a few, mostly advanced industrialized host economies, MNCs will face local firms who are themselves MNCs in which case the productivity gap will be narrower. Often these firms are competing in monopolistically competitive product markets.

interests between separate firms that generate risk because interests of parent firms and their foreign affiliates are aligned.[7]

2.1.2   What Firms Become Multinational Corporations?

MNCs are far from a random sample of firms. They are among the world's most efficient producers in their respective industries. Firms that ultimately become multinational start out with highly productive firm-specific assets. They may produce high quality cars, innovative pharmaceutical drugs, or lower cost telecommunications services. Firms that eventually become MNCs are ex-ante more productive than their domestic counterparts, and once they become multinational they register additional productivity gains (Barba Navaretti and Falzoni 2004).

Firms vary in their preference for control over specific assets; only the most productive firms pursue FDI. As noted some firms do pursue international technology-licensing agreements and supplier-producer relationships. The firms that turn to FDI are the most sensitive to contracting risks. Technological sophistication, highly correlated with productivity, usually makes firms more sensitive to contracting risks because expected losses in the event of contract breach are higher. These firms choose FDI over less costly alternatives in order to retain control over their specific assets. The alternatives leave firms open to theft or degradation of their assets and to holdup.

Relative to these alternatives, FDI is costly for firms. These costs include the establishment, coordination, and monitoring of multiple production facilities in unfamiliar countries that are often at a great physical distance. Foreign-owned firms also typically have less information about the local market than their domestic counterparts, placing them at a disadvantage. MNCs initially know less about potential suppliers, distributional channels, consumer tastes, or other tacit information needed to operate in the local market. MNCs have less certainty about their expected income. They must contend with economic volatility, such as currency fluctuations, and political risks such as regulatory changes. Due to these costs, the firms that select FDI are among the world's most efficient producers. MNCs are productive enough that FDI is profitable despite its high cost.

---

[7]   Specifically, MNCs resolve incomplete contracting problems by allocating residual rights of control, those rights that are not ex-ante contractable, to the parent firm (Grossman and Hart 1986).

The intangible quality of firm-specific assets generates economies of scale for firms. Economies of scale are the cost savings that firms create by expanding their production. Firms face high costs when they initially develop assets. These costs include research and development and marketing to establish brand reputation. These costs are fixed and constitute a large fraction of total production costs. Consider the production of computer software. A software firm faces high fixed costs to developing the software including the cost of employing computer programmers and the computing equipment that the programmers use. Once the software is ready for sale, the firm has virtually no marginal cost, that is, the cost of producing each additional unit is trivial. A consumer who buys the software is paying a portion of the initial fixed cost. The software firm's optimal strategy is to sell as many units as possible in order to spread these fixed costs across as many consumers as possible. By expanding production, the firm can lower the cost of each unit of software it sells.

FDI allows firms to expand internationally in order to maximize economies of scale that arise from their intangible assets.[8] The additional productivity gains following FDI reflect the firms' higher economies of scale. Helpman, Melitz, and Yeaple (2004) find that multinational exporting firms are, on average, 15 percent more productive than nonmultinational firms that export. This finding attests to the additional productivity of MNCs, above and beyond that of firms that are productive enough to compete in international markets. To reiterate, there are alternatives for capturing scale economies but they entail the contracting risks described above. In place of investment to manufacture production inputs in foreign countries, firms could instead rely upon separate foreign suppliers to provide low-cost inputs. Similarly, firms could take advantage of foreign market opportunities by licensing their specific assets to firms in those markets. MNCs are so productive that they can profitably undertake FDI and bypass contracting risks.

To understand how FDI affects recipient countries' economies, it matters that the MNC is usually much more productive than the top local firms. To be sure, both trade and FDI expose the recipient country's economy to competition from the world's most productive producers. Trade introduce goods and services that embody their producers' advantages. FDI introduces the technology necessary to produce goods and services. FDI openness, however, exposes recipient countries to more international competition than

---

[8] Brainard (1997) finds that the firms most likely to pursue FDI are those with high firm-level scale economies but low plant-level scale economies because FDI potentially sacrifices production scale economies from concentrating production in one place.

trade openness, because FDI occurs in industries that produce nontradables. These are typically services industries in which products cannot be stored or transported.

MNCs can enter foreign markets in several ways: by establishing a new firm as a subsidiary, greenfield investment, or through a merger and acquisition (M&A) by acquiring a previously existing firm. In fact, most global FDI occurs through M&As, and this is mostly driven by M&As between industrialized countries. In 2000, 76 percent of all FDI occurred by M&A, making up 89 percent of total FDI into advanced economies but only 36 percent of FDI in developing countries (Barba Navaretti and Venables 2004).

Because M&As dominate as a method of FDI, a rival explanation for the MNCs' observed productivity advantage is that they select the most productive existing firms to acquire. If so, then FDI would simply shift ownership rights of existing assets to a foreigner without adding any value to the recipient country's economy. In fact, studies of MNC-acquired firms show that while MNCs do choose the most productive of local firms to acquire, the acquired firms' labor productivity and sales rise significantly *after* acquisition.. There are several causes of these productivity gains, including the adoption of MNCs' technology and production practices, cheaper financing through the parent company, and an increase in the firms' scale of production, particularly greater production for export (Arnold and Javorcik 2009, Guadalupe, Kuzmina, and Thomas 2012). Thus, the basic stylized fact that MNCs are more productive than host country firms holds even though MNCs tend to select exceptionally productive firms for acquisition.

MNCs' superior productivity is a critical fact in the derivation of FDI's distributive effects. In Chapter 3 I derive the consequences of FDI inflows for wages and local firms' returns. I treat FDI inflows as the entry of firms that are more productive than local firms. MNCs' productivity advantages allow them to pay higher wages and raise competition in product markets. The next section describes the sources of variation in how these advantages manifest in recipient countries.

2.1.3 Export-Oriented versus Market-Oriented FDI: The Organization of Multinational Production

Like all forms of international capital flows, FDI is ultimately a strategy by which capital owners seek higher returns on their assets. How FDI generates these returns, however, are quite different from those of more liquid forms of capital. In the presence of capital mobility, flows of financial capital follow the logic of factor price equalization: capital owners in capital-rich economies transfer their assets to capital-poor economies where, due to the relative scarcity of capital, a higher rental rate for capital prevails. By leveraging cross-national differences in the price of capital, owners of liquid capital flows earn returns. In contrast, owners of firm-specific capital cannot earn returns by directly lending their capital because markets often do not exist for the direct sale and purchase of firm-specific capital.[9] Even where such markets do exist, many firms are unwilling to use them because of the multiple incomplete contracting problems that they present.

Unlike portfolio capital flows, FDI yields returns on firm-specific assets *indirectly* in product markets. Although MNCs are uniformly productive, they vary in how they organize production across their foreign affiliates. Some MNCs organize production internationally to lower production costs by arbitraging cross-national differences in production costs and selling products outside of the host country. I refer to this form of investment as *exported-oriented FDI*. Other MNCs organize production in order to compete in foreign product markets. This form of FDI is called *market-oriented FDI*.[10]

Each organizational form entails different patterns for organizing production across countries. MNCs pursuing export-oriented FDI fragment the production process across countries. They maintain "headquarter" functions like research, development, and marketing in the home country and relocate production activities to countries with lower production costs.[11] Most often, lower production costs come from lower labor costs, but the cost of other inputs like electricity and raw materials also factor into a firm's calculations. In this form of FDI, MNCs export what their foreign subsidiaries produce out of the host country for sale in either the home market or a third country.

---

[9] Indeed, FDI inflows do not systematically influence the supply of liquid capital in recipient countries. MNCs may transfer cash into the host country to finance their investments but they can also borrow money within the host country. It is for this reason that many criticize estimates of FDI inflows derived from national balance-of-payments statistics as an inaccurate measure of economic activity (Beugelsdijk, Hennart, Slangen, and Smeets 2010).

[10] There are finer-grained distinctions in the motives for FDI and the organization of multinational production, but they can all be accurately classified into one of these two categories based on whether production in the host country is intended for export or local sale. For example, "export-platform FDI" is export-oriented FDI located in a region of the world with multiple possible markets. Firms produce goods and export them from the host country to other countries in the region.

[11] Helpman (1984) was the first to describe this motive for FDI.

The foreign investments of U.S. semiconductor firms illustrate salient features of export-oriented FDI. Semiconductor devices conduct electricity through a set of tightly integrated circuits and are the backbone of modern electronics. Semiconductor production is ideal for export-oriented FDI because production is separated into four discrete stages: design, fabrication, assembly, and testing. In addition, the cost of transporting semiconductors is only 1.5–2 percent of the product value (Grunwald and Flamm 1985, 49).[12] The industry was an early adopter of export-oriented FDI due to intense price competition among producers. In 1961, U.S.-based Fairchild Semiconductor established the first overseas semiconductor assembly plant in Hong Kong. Assembly entails bonding electrical leads to a silicon wafer. All major American semiconductor producers followed Fairchild abroad, establishing subsidiaries in several developing countries including Malaysia, Singapore, Hong Kong, South Korea, Mexico, and multiple Caribbean nations. By the mid-1970s, these overseas assembly plants could assemble a single device for $1.50, half of the unit assembly cost in the United States (Yoffie 1993, 201). By 1978, more than 80 percent of semiconductor devices sold in the United States were assembled and tested abroad.

The semiconductor example illustrates not only firms' motivation for investment as a cost-saving measure but also how that motive dictates the organization of multinational production. There are positive returns to relocating production abroad when a firm can site segments of the production process in countries abundant in the necessary factor inputs.

Export-oriented investments flow to countries abundant in the factors used intensively in production and with whom trade costs – transport costs and trade barriers – are low enough to allow production inputs and final products to move across borders at minimal cost (Hanson, Mataloni, Slaughter 2003, Yeaple 2003).[13] Consistent with these motives, export-oriented FDI by U.S.-based MNCs in the 1990s was most common in electronics, transportation equipment, and industrial machinery. Canada and Mexico were the primary destinations for these investments. East Asia was

---

[12] The industry used manual assembly rather than automated techniques because automation would have required large capital investments. The exceptionally fast pace of technological change in the industry (typically production runs lasted only two to three years) rendered automation technologies obsolete quickly.

[13] But see the debate between Carr, Markusen, and Maskus (2001, 2003) and Blonigen, Davies, and Head (2003) on the relative importance of export and market-seeking motives in explaining aggregate FDI flows.

a common site for electronics production and assembly (Hanson, Mataloni, and Slaughter 2001). In these examples, it is evident how MNCs exploit the geographic proximity of their home countries to countries with lower production costs. Proximity minimizes transport costs of production inputs and finished products moving between the home and host countries. Due to the need for trade in inputs and products, export-oriented FDI and trade are complements.

By contrast, MNCs pursuing market-oriented FDI replicate production facilities in multiple countries to produce goods and services for sale within the host's product market (Markusen 1984). Trade and market-oriented FDI are substitutes rather than complements. MNCs organize production in this manner when less expensive means of competing in foreign markets are unavailable. There are two main impediments to trade that prompt MNCs to pursue market-oriented FDI: tariff-jumping and trade costs.[14] Market-oriented FDI is sometimes referred to as tariff-jumping FDI, because historically it has been a way to bypass tariff barriers in order to enter a protected foreign market.[15]

FDI by Japanese automobile firms into the United States in the 1980s illustrates the characteristics of market-oriented FDI. By end of the 1970s, U.S. carmakers faced growing competition from Japanese imports. Amid a deep recession punctuated by high oil prices, American consumers increasingly favored Japanese cars for their low cost and relatively high fuel efficiency. In response to the calls of U.S. automakers for greater protection, the United States negotiated with Japan a voluntary export restraint that capped Japanese auto imports at 1.68 million vehicles annually. In response to these trade barriers, Japanese auto producers established U.S. manufacturing plants in locations like Marysville, Ohio (Honda) and Smyrna, Tennessee (Nissan). In its first year of production, 1985, Honda's Ohio plant manufactured 150,000 cars per year. By the end of the 1980s, eight Japanese carmakers had established U.S. production facilities. In 1991 North American

---

[14] I emphasize tariffs, but many forms of regulation can prompt firms to circumvent with market-oriented FDI. MNCs may also make market-oriented investments in order to customize products to suit local tastes (Thomas 2011).

[15] Some countries impose trade barriers for the very purpose of attracting FDI in the tradition of state-led development strategies. Bhagwati et al. (1992) go so far as to argue that some MNCs invest to diffuse the pressure for protectionist trade policies in host countries. See however Blonigen and Figlio (1998) for the opposite finding that autos and textiles FDI in a U.S. congressional district increases the likelihood of that district's representative voting for tariffs.

affiliates of Japanese automakers produced 17 percent of all cars and light trucks produced in the region; all of these vehicles were sold within North America (Chung, Mitchell, and Yeung 2003).

MNCs prefer to invest in large host markets in order to achieve economies of scale large enough to recoup the fixed costs of investment. The example of Japanese firms' investments into the U.S. automobile sector demonstrates this. U.S. affiliates initially imported all components from their Japanese suppliers, but within a decade a majority of their inputs were American-made. Japanese parts suppliers established U.S. affiliates to serve Japanese automakers with whom they had a relationship (Levinsohn 1997).[16] The large size of the North American auto market allowed the Japanese firms to capture high economies of scale.[17]

MNCs also make market-oriented investments in response to high trade costs. When the physical costs of transporting a product across borders exceeds a firm's expected return, market-oriented FDI is a possible alternative. In practice, this motive for market-oriented FDI is most evident in the services sector. Services are commodities that are usually nontradable, because they require geographic proximity between producer and consumer. At the end of the twentieth century, roughly 60 percent of FDI flows were in services industries (UNCTAD 2004). Although the service sector is a broad and heterogeneous category of economic activity,[18] any service entails the simultaneous production and consumption of an economic activity, and producer and consumer are often in close physical proximity. For example, consider haircuts. A haircut must be simultaneously produced and consumed; it cannot be stored. Similarly, producer and consumer must be in very close physical proximity, because haircuts cannot be transported separately from the parties to the transaction. For all intents and purposes,

---

[16] The relative appreciation of the Japanese yen vis-à-vis the U.S. dollar also made it more efficient to source parts within the United States.

[17] More precisely, market-oriented investments are likely when firms have high firm-level scale economies (usually a function of intangible assets) but low plant-level scale economies. Brainard 1997 demonstrates this empirically.

[18] The International Standard Industrial Classification (ISIC), the United Nations' classification of industries, identifies ten broad categories of service industries: electricity, gas, and water supply; construction; wholesale and retail trade; hotels and restaurants; transport, storage, and communication; financial intermediation; real estate, renting, and business activities; education; health and social work; and other community, social, and personal service activities. These categories are from ISIC Revision 3. The complete classification, including full descriptions of each category, can be found at: http://unstats.un.org/unsd/cr/registry/regcst.asp?Cl=17

services cannot be traded at arm's length across borders.[19] MNCs use market-oriented investments to produce and sell services in close proximity to foreign consumers. FDI in conjunction with privatization in sectors like telecommunications and energy fueled much of the growth in services FDI at the end of the twentieth century.

These organizational forms are not mutually exclusive. A single MNC can have some foreign affiliates that produce for export and others that produce and sell output in the host market. Market-oriented FDI in services account for the majority of total FDI flows, but export-oriented FDI as a proportion of total FDI has grown over time. More importantly, some manufacturing industries that used to make mostly market-oriented investments have shifted increasingly toward export-oriented investment. The computer-hardware industry illustrates this transformation. Figure 2.1 graphs the percent of all US-based MNCs sales made outside of the country of production. In 1977, the leftmost point on the graph, 30 percent of all foreign affiliate sales occurred outside of the host country. A full 70 percent of U.S. computer-hardware MNCs' output was sold in the country in which the MNC manufactured it, illustrating the dominance of market-oriented FDI. By 2000 the proportions had reversed: 73 percent of total affiliate sales took place outside the country in which the product was manufactured. This dramatic reversal illustrates how MNCs restructured production over this period. More recent estimates for all multinationals confirm this pattern. By 2005, 46 percent of all multinational affiliates' sales occurred outside of the country in which the product was made (Alfaro and Charlton 2009).

The emergence of export-oriented FDI is part of a larger trend of vertical specialization, a fragmentation of the production process across multiple locations. This specialization has increased cross-border trade of intermediate production inputs. Intrafirm trade is vertical trade that occurs between foreign affiliates of the same multinational firm. In 2000, intrafirm trade as a percentage of total U.S. trade grew to more than 80 percent; there are similar estimates of vertical trade for other industrialized countries.[20] To illustrate, consider Mexico's maquiladoras, manufacturing facilities that

---

[19] This refers to cross-border trade in services rather than the more general meaning of "trade in services" enshrined in the WTO's General Agreement on Trade in Services. Technology has made some inroads in weakening these constraints on cross-border trade, but they continue to hold for most services.

[20] See Bernard, Jensen, and Schott (2009, 537–538) for U.S. estimates; Hummels, Ishii, and Yi (2001) for descriptions of OECD trade patterns.

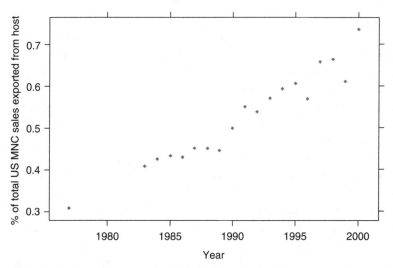

Figure 2.1 Growth in export-oriented FDI in U.S. computer-hardware MNCs, 1977–2000.

Note: Figure plots sales data for U.S.-based multinational firms in the computing and office machines industry (in 1999–2000: the industry was classified as "computers and peripheral equipment"). Points represent, for each year, the percent of all sales by these firms that were made outside of the host country in which goods were produced. This is a standard metric of the export-orientation of FDI. Data are from *Annual Survey of Direct Investment Abroad* compiled by the Bureau of Economic Analysis, U.S. Department of Commerce.

import production inputs, primarily from the United States, on a tariff-free basis, and produce exclusively for export back to the U.S. market. This arrangement allows U.S. firms to take advantage of lower production costs in Mexico. Many developing countries have created similar programs to attract export-oriented investments. Export-oriented FDI grew with the passage of the U.S.-Canada Free Trade Agreement, which later expanded into the North American Free Trade Agreement to include Mexico.

As trade costs have declined, export-oriented investments became more appealing to multinational firms. Trade costs are all of the transactions costs associated with cross-border trade including transport costs (e.g. shipping, insurance) and policies like trade restrictions that raise the cost of products sold in foreign markets. Figure 2.2 shows that the growth in worldwide trade preceded growth in total FDI inflows. The panels divided by country income level demonstrate that the trend is consistent across all income levels. This data suggest that growth in world trade may account for part of the explosive growth of FDI in the mid-1990s. The precipitous decline in communications costs also contributed to the rise of multi-country production

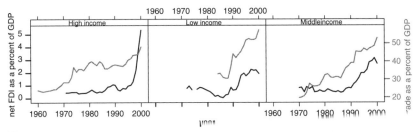

Figure 2.2 Trade and FDI flows by country income group, 1960–2000.
Note: Each panel of this graph shows trade and percentage of GDP and FDI as a percentage of GDP for one of three country income groups. Data and country income classifications are from the World Bank's World Development Indicators.

networks by lowering coordination costs (Portes and Rey 2005). Parallel to trade liberalization countries have strengthened foreign-owned firms' property rights through national legislation, bilateral investment treaties, and investment clauses in trade agreements.

Variation in the organization of multinational production creates distinct distributive effects in recipient countries. The crucial difference between market- and export-oriented FDI is the absence of market competition in export-oriented investments. MNCs still produce but do so for export rather than to compete with local producers. The only cost to local firms of export-oriented FDI is the increase in production costs due to greater demand for inputs like labor. This difference helps to explain cross-industry variation in the incidence of FDI regulation. All else equal, the lower cost to local firms of export-oriented FDI reduces local firms' incentives to lobby for restrictions.

2.2 The Distributive Effects of FDI Inflows: Implications of the Specific Factors Model

The specific factors model as applied to FDI begins from different priors than its standard applications to trade and portfolio capital flows. Unlike trade and portfolio capital, FDI's distributive effects does not depend on host countries' relative factor endowments or technological advantages. Firms motivated to engage in FDI, especially market-seeking FDI, do not heavily weigh host country factor endowments.[21] Although labor cost

---

[21] See Helpman (2006) on the relative importance of factor abundance/comparative advantage and firm organizational choices in driving FDI flows.

savings motivate export-oriented investments, MNCs' production requirements are sufficiently varied that FDI does not systematically flow into
conventionally-defined labor-abundant countries (Carr, Markusen, and
Maskus 2003, Yeaple 2003). Accordingly, in applying the specific factors
model to FDI, I assume that FDI's distributive effects are the same, regardless of recipient countries' factor endowments. For example, FDI raises
labor demand in labor-abundant countries just as much as it does in labor-
scarce countries.

The specific factors model provides a stylized illustration of FDI's distributive effects by highlighting how factor groups' respective incomes respond
to exogenous changes in the amount of productive capital present in the
economy.[22] The model consists of two industries and three factors: productive capital specific to each industry and labor that is mobile across industries.[23] Both industries produce a commodity using their specific capital
and labor as inputs. This is an apt model, because FDI inflows "transmit
equity capital, entrepreneurship, and technological or other productive
knowledge in an industry-specific package" (Caves 1971, 3).[24] The model
yields FDI's distributive effects by considering an increase in the supply of
one industry's capital stock.

FDI inflows raise wages by increasing labor demand. The increase in
one industry's specific capital raises the marginal revenue product of labor
employed in that industry. Profit-maximizing firms hire additional workers
to the point that marginal revenue product is again equal to commodity price.
This expansion necessitates a rise in wages to draw workers into the industry.
Because labor is mobile across industries, this expansion comes at the expense
of other firms who must raise wages to retain workers. These wage increases
come at the expense of returns to local capital owners.[25] Both export and market-oriented FDI raise wages by increasing labor demand. If we assume that
FDI does not change local commodity prices, as is true of export-oriented
FDI, these changes do not alter each factor group's buying power.

---

[22] Jones (1971). Unlike trade there are no widely agreed upon general equilibrium models of
FDI flows that specify the distributional effects of FDI inflows. See Carr, Markusen, and
Maskus (2001) and Blonigen, Davies, and Head (2003) for discussion of the controversies
surrounding such models.

[23] The model also assumes the full employment of all factors, and that firms are price-
takers.

[24] See Grossman and Helpman (1996) for a discussion of FDI policy preferences with industry specific labor. See also Batra and Ramachandran (1980) for a similar model of FDI's
distributional effects and Brown and Stern (2001) for a general equilibrium model of FDI
restrictions.

[25] The cost to local capital owners is increasing in the relative labor intensity of production.

In the context of my model, market-oriented FDI is the equivalent of both an increase in one industry's capital and a reduction in the commodity price of that industry's output. Firms make market-oriented investments when other, less costly, forms of market entry are unavailable. Given these motives of horizontal FDI, it is reasonable to infer that it occurs in commodity markets in which there is a wedge between world and local prices. Expanded production in the FDI-receiving sector generates greater supply of its associated commodity, triggering a decline in price and competing away existing firms' product market rents. Through heightened competition, market-oriented FDI is a second mechanism leading to the decline of returns to local firms following FDI into their industry.[26]

2.2.1 Accounting for Alternate Mechanisms

Some may object that the specific factors model is too parsimonious to capture FDI's complex effects on recipient countries and that an expanded model that incorporates these nuances could yield different predictions regarding FDI's distributive effects. In this section, I discuss four ways through which these alternate effects could run counter to the model's predictions. Although there is some evidence supporting these alternate mechanisms, they do not, on average, yield different configurations of distributive effects. Chapter 4 confirms empirically that the predictions of the basic specific factors model regarding labor hold. Chapter 6 does the same for local capital preferences.

First, some industry characteristics can blunt the negative effects of FDI inflows for local firms. The specific factors model assumes perfectly competitive industries whose firms have constant returns to scale production functions and that, within an industry, firms' output are perfect substitutes. In practice, however, FDI occurs in monopolistically competitive industries in which firms have increasing returns to their production scale. FDI is also common in industries with distinct varieties of products that are imperfect substitutes for the products of other firms in the same industry.

Domestic firms in these industries face losses from FDI inflows in the manner predicted by the specific factors model but they are potentially lower than the losses of firms in perfectly competitive industries. In

---

[26] The implication of commodity price changes for wages hinges on labor's consumption preferences, ranging from neutral to positive. Recall that firms minimize unit costs in selecting their production inputs. Jones (1971, 7) notes "the change in the market price of [the commodity] must be a positively weighted average of (and therefore trapped between) the changes in individual factor prices."

monopolistically competitive industries firms' profits, their markups above marginal cost, are inversely correlated with the number of producers in the market (Helpman and Krugman 1985). The entry of new firms introduces new product varieties into the market, lowering demand for existing varieties, all else equal. Existing firms, facing lower demand, reduce production. These firms face higher average total costs owing to the lower scale of production, amounting to a reduction in profit. The precise loss to domestic producers depends on the degree of product differentiation in an industry, making product differentiation an important industry characteristic to determining the magnitude of FDI's costs to local producers.

Second, if there are positive productivity spillovers from MNCs to local firms, those spillovers could reverse local firms into supporters of unrestricted FDI inflows. To the extent that there are positive productivity spillovers, FDI could complement rather than substitute for local firms. Theoretically, FDI generates positive spillovers for local firms by introducing highly productive technologies. Productivity spillovers to local firms can occur in many ways. Local firms hire workers previously employed by the MNC who introduce productivity enhancements acquired within the foreign-owned firm. Local firms observe MNCs' production in close proximity and reverse engineer their technologies. Local firms also gain access to lower cost/higher quality production inputs produced by the MNC. In some cases, an MNC assists a local firm in raising its quality standards sufficiently to be a local supplier (Javorcik 2004, Sembenelli and Siotis 2008, Javorcik and Sparternau 2011). None of these spillover mechanisms occur because of government regulation.[27]

In order to reverse the prediction of the specific factors model, however, local firms, on average, would have to anticipate a net increase in productivity due to spillovers that exceeds the higher labor costs and product market competition. In Chapter 6 I demonstrate that these factors do not flip local capital FDI preferences. Empirical analysis of industry-level variation includes controls for product differentiation, industry concentration, and the research and development capacity to capture possible productivity spillovers.

Third, the specific factors model does not account for two possible ways in which FDI inflows could lower expected wages and therefore the probability of labor support for unrestricted FDI: (1) greater employment volatility and (2) a net reduction in labor demand through use of more

---

[27] Additionally, spillovers are contingent on the host country's absorptive capacity such as human capital stocks (Borensztein, DeGrigorio, and Lee 1998) and financial development (Alfaro, Chanda, Kalemli-Ozcan, and Sayek 2004).

capital-intensive production technologies.[28] If these effects subsume those described above, labor may oppose FDI inflows. Theoretically MNCs' labor demand is more elastic than that of domestic firms, because MNCs can more readily reallocate production across multiple countries than purely domestic firms (Owen forthcoming). Although evidence of volatility is mixed (Barba Navaretti, Checchi, and Turrini 2003) survey evidence indicates that labor detests this source of job insecurity (Scheve and Slaughter 2004).[29] There are, however, instances in which FDI affords greater job security relative to employment in local firms, particularly through MNCs' expansions during economic crises (Aguiar and Gopinath 2005, Desai, Foley, and Forbes 2008).

FDI inflows may lower net labor demand, inasmuch as MNCs replace labor with more capital-intensive production technologies. This concern is especially great when MNCs acquire an existing host country firm and integrate it into its larger multi-country production network. MNCs might shed parts of the acquired firm to eliminate duplicate functions to take full advantage of economies of scale. Privatization is a special case of foreign acquisition in which workers also stand to lose the perks of public employment (Branstetter and Feenstra 2002). Here too there is mixed empirical evidence on FDI's net effect on labor demand: while there is net job loss following some acquisitions, in other cases MNCs expand production after acquisition to meet higher product demand (Arnold and Javorcik 2009).[30] In Chapter 4 I show that these labor market conditions in which FDI can occur do not diminish average labor support for FDI. Models of individual-level preferences for FDI include controls for respondents' subjective sense of job security and public sector employment.

Fourth, those familiar with existing applications of specific factors models to trade may wonder about FDI's distributive effects when both labor and capital are specific to an industry. In the trade context, studies find

---

[28] Some might argue that FDI reduces labor welfare through the use of exploitive labor practices. In practice MNCs adhere to core labor practices more strongly than local firms and countries with higher average labor practices receive higher volumes of FDI (Mosley 2010, Brown, Deardorff, and Stern 2003, Kucera 2002, Rodrik 1996). This pattern is consistent with MNCs' relatively high demand for skilled labor.

[29] Many studies do find that foreign firms adjust more quickly to shocks than domestic firms, which can account for the perception of less job security among MNC employees.

[30] More precisely the effect of FDI on labor demand depends on the price elasticity of demand for the product. In the case of export-oriented FDI, production is for the world market. Thus, output is not constrained by the size of the host market so the introduction of laborsaving technologies should not reduce net labor demand. In market-oriented FDI, this is a possibility only when local product demand is sufficiently price inelastic that demand remains constant following a price reduction.

that when both labor and capital are industry-specific, they share the same
policy preferences, because returns for both types of factors depend on the
same industry's performance. In the FDI context, however, the opposite it
true. The more specific factors are to the same industry, the more their FDI
preferences diverge. In this scenario, FDI inflows still raise labor demand
but it would be for industry-specific labor. Industry-specific labor should be
more likely to support FDI inflows than mobile labor because as a smaller
pool of qualified labor the expected returns to FDI should be higher than
when MNCs use mobile labor (Grossman and Helpman 1996).[31] In short,
labor specificity only magnifies labor's gains from unrestricted FDI inflows.
Similarly, FDI's effects on consumer welfare can only reinforce the division between labor and capital. Labor experiences real, rather than nominal wage increases because product prices are either fixed, as in the case of
export-oriented, or decline due to greater market competition.[32]

2.3 FDI Preferences: Increased Labor Demand and Returns to Skills

The specific factors model implies that labor is more likely to support unrestricted FDI inflows in anticipation of expected wage increases following
MNCs' entry into their market.[33] A wealth of evidence shows that wages
do in fact rise following FDI across a variety of industries in both industrialized and emerging economies.[34] Most studies find a wage premium of

[31] In a model with both industry-specific capital and labor the only difference in distributive effects from those outlined here is that capital's opposition to FDI would be confined
to its own industry because there is no intersectoral labor movement in response to FDI
inflows.

[32] Consumption-based theories as applied to trade policy preferences get traction from a
decrease in factor prices coupled with an increase in consumer welfare: support for trade
can be attributed to consumption preferences when factor income is expected to decline
(Baker 2005). FDI cannot yield this configuration of income effects; wages rise regardless
of the relative abundance of labor in the host country. Consumption effects range from
neutral for export-oriented FDI to positive for market-oriented investments. For the purposes of this study, this means that factor price and product price effects cannot be disen-
tangled as independent sources of labor's FDI preferences. Theoretically, price collusion
between MNCs and local firms is possible. In practice asymmetries in the two groups' cost
structure makes sustained collusion difficult.

[33] There are other, related reasons for MNCs' higher wages including their use of efficiency
wages to mitigate high search costs and profit-sharing between parent firms' and their foreign affiliates (Budd, Konings, and Slaughter 2005).

[34] See Lipsey (2002) for a comprehensive review of evidence on the labor market effects of
FDI inflows. Key country studies include those by Haddad and Harrison (1993), Harrison
(1996), Aitken, Harrison, and Lipsey (1996), and Barry (2004).

10 percent to 30 percent for unskilled production workers in foreign-owned manufacturing firms. In many developing countries, existing local firms pay higher wages after the entry of a foreign-owned firm despite constant or declining productivity (Görg and Greenway 2001). This result demonstrates that rising wages in local firms are not due to positive productivity spillovers from MNCs to local firms.[35]

We observe particularly large wage increases for skilled labor following FDI. MNCs have greater demand for skilled labor because of the relative sophistication of their production technologies. Not only do MNCs tend to operate in more technologically advanced industries but also their production technologies demand a higher skill level than their typical host country counterparts. Consider variation in production technologies across auto firms. Multinational auto producers automate production by using robots to weld and assemble cars. Less advanced producers rely on labor to manually perform the same tasks (Moran 2002, 288–289). The former requires skilled labor to operate and maintain robotic devices whereas the latter calls for basic manual assembly and welding skills. It is estimated that MNC skilled-labor wages are as much as 50 percent to 70 percent higher than skilled-labor wages paid by local firms (Haddad and Harrison 1993, Lipsey and Sjöholm 2002). FDI was the single largest source of increases in skilled-labor wages in Mexico during the 1980s (Feenstra and Hanson 1997).

Based on this exceptionally strong empirical finding, I draw the further hypothesis that, while all labor stands to benefit from FDI due to expected wage increases, support for unrestricted FDI varies by skill level. Skilled workers are more likely to support FDI inflows because their anticipated wage increases are higher. These higher expected gains to skilled labor reflect the fact that MNCs, by virtue of their advanced production technologies, are more likely to require more skilled labor in the production process. In Chapter 4 I test this claim using survey data from seventeen Latin American countries and variety of skill measures. I confirm that across skill levels, labor supports FDI and that, on average, labor support is more likely at higher skill levels.

These findings are robust to controls for alternate explanations of FDI preferences. Empirical analyses include controls for other possible economic

---

[35] One concern in drawing inferences from this evidence is that MNCs acquire firms that were ex-ante more productive. If this were the case an observation of higher wages in foreign-owned firm could simply be an artifact of selection rather than a consequence of rising labor demand. A growing number of studies use firm-level panel data to control for unobserved firm characteristics and conclude that MNCs raise productivity levels even in those plants they acquire. See Lipsey and Sjöholm (2002).

consequences including FDI fueled job insecurity, privatization. Further, I investigate the role of non-economic factors like nationalist sentiment in the formation of preferences.

2.4 Sources of Cross-National Variation: Political Regime Type

Less developed countries had higher average levels of ownership regulations than advanced industrialized countries for most of the sample period 1970–2000. Less developed countries by definition have more labor than capital, and therefore most people in those countries stood to gain from FDI. If so, why did those countries restrict foreign ownership the most? The answer is that political regime type (democracy or autocracy) shaped politicians' responses to labor and capital's opposing policy preferences about FDI.

Political regime type is a summary characterization of institutional features like the structure of representation, the division of policymaking authority among elected officials, the length of politicians' tenure, and the conditions of leader turnover (Jaggers and Marshall 2004, Cheibub, Gandhi, Vreeland 2009). Democracies are regimes in which these institutional features foster politicians' accountability to voters. In autocracies, institutional features, or the absence thereof, leave policymakers' authority unchecked. This distinction between democracy and autocracy matters, because it corresponds to the size of the population that has political representation and thus to which leaders are accountable. In democracies, leaders are accountable to a broad swath of the population through universal franchise and regular elections. In autocracies, a small subset of the population de facto "selects" leaders outside of the parameters of transparent and inclusive procedures (Bueno de Mesquita, Smith, Siverson, and Morrow 2004).

Local capital in autocracies most commonly takes the form of a nascent industrial class that furnished support to leaders in exchange for favorable economic policies. In some cases industrial interests are politically aligned but formally separate, as in South Korea, but in other cases like Indonesia and Turkey political leaders profited directly from industrial interests (Granovetter 1995).[36] Firms connected to ruling politicians have higher profits due to their preferential access to financing, information, and opportunities (Faccio 2006, Mitton 2008, Fisman 2001). Local capital owners

---

[36] These relationships are not static. To the extent that there are factions within autocratic governments and among industrial groups, groups and politicians' interests can diverge. Siegel (2007) provides detailed evidence for South Korea. Khanna and Yefeh (2007) argue this to be the case in Indonesia and Malaysia.

used their influence with policymakers to secure FDI policies favorable to their interests. During the period of active industrialization in Taiwan, the National Council of Industry and Commerce, a group representing the country's largest business groups, had privileged access to policymakers. Weekly meetings provided a forum to communicate economic needs and priorities (Fields 1997). Deep informal connections cement relationships whether they are through shared ethnic, geographic, or institutional ties. For example, patterns in South Korea show that graduates of the same elite regional high schools support mutual business and political interests (Siegel 2007). These linkages, coupled with patterns of highly concentrated industrial ownership, as will be described in Chapter 3, lowered collective action costs that would arise if there were multiple firms seeking MNC partnerships.

Particularly in the area of FDI, there was close coordination among leaders and local industrial interests. Evans (1979) famously described a triple alliance between MNCs, the state, and local capital owners. Evans and Gereffi (1981) argued that the relatively low penetration of wholly owned MNCs into Mexico's largest firms is evidence of local capital's political connections. Countries maintained tight controls over FDI and actively paired up MNCs with local partners. In South Korea, a central body called the Economic Planning Board screened all proposed investments and paired MNCs with local firms. This structure allowed bureaucrats to integrate FDI policies with the overall approach to economic development. Even the export-led economies of East Asia, long associated with a heavy presence of foreign firms, actually imposed severe restrictions on FDI. The formal restrictions are an understatement. There was informal scrutiny of "technologies to be transferred, the royalties associated with those technologies, personnel policies, the extent of local procurement and sales, and the implications of the project for exports" (Haggard 1990, 199). Likewise, Mexico's National Commission on Foreign Investment exercised control over which foreign-owned firms were allowed to enter the country.

Democratization provides the impetus for FDI liberalization by orienting policymakers' incentives toward generating political support from labor. Democratization can empower labor in multiple ways. In some cases, democratization makes it easier for labor to lobby for preferred policies.[37] Consistent with these political changes, Rodrik (1999) showed that democratization in this period resulted in higher manufacturing wages and corresponded to higher value-added in the manufacturing sector contributed by

[37] See Stokes (2001).

labor. He concluded that these shifts were due to expanded political representation rather than more specific labor rights like the right to organize.[38]

Similarly, labor unions show greater interest in attracting FDI than they did during authoritarian rule. In the absence of political rights unions could not adequately bargain with MNCs over the terms of employment. Under the protections afforded by democracy, unions have greater bargaining leverage to capture potential gains from FDI. Guillén (2000a) documented this shift among South Korean, Argentine, and Spanish labor unions following democratization. In all three countries, labor opposed FDI when their countries were under autocratic rule. Labor reversed its position after democratization; the extent of labor's support for FDI correlates with the extent of democratization.[39] Of the three countries, according to Guillén, Spain's labor unions embraced FDI the most, because their country's shift to democracy was the most extensive. Spanish labor unions actively participated in attracting MNC investments in the 1980s. To be sure, union varied within and across countries in how open they were to FDI, but on average labor's rising political stock coincided with a stronger preference in support of FDI inflows. In some countries, labor groups themselves fomented regime change by organizing paralyzing general strikes and mass protests that destabilized authoritarian regimes, or by spearheading broad social movements to demand faster and more extensive political liberalization (Collier and Mahoney 1997).[40]

In addition to direct lobbying by labor interests, there are other ways through which democratization produces FDI liberalization. Democratization entails contested elections, subjecting leaders to regular approval from this expanded electorate. In the absence of direct pressure,

---

[38] Adding to these gains was a change in the types of FDI countries received. Ownership liberalization prompted more export-oriented FDI that draws on a wider skill range of the workforce, like maquiladoras, and brought cutting-edge technologies where firms located segments of a multi-country production process.

[39] The subset of workers employed by state-owned firms stand to lose from liberalization. Chapter 5 tests the implications of this point for FDI preferences.

[40] In Mexico, Venezuela, and Argentina there was, to varying degrees, a long-standing alliance between labor-oriented political parties and labor unions (Murillo 2001). This alliance made it to the mutual benefit of both parties to maintain the relationship: the parties provided unions benefits for which union leaders could take credit and use to maintain their leadership position within the union vis-à-vis challengers. The political leaders received the support of unions and their members in return. This mutual dependency explains why labor unions did not vigorously protest neoliberal economic reforms (needed to maintain loyalty to politicians) but also why reforms did not typically include reforms of the labor market (a concession to the unions by the politicians to maintain their support).

democratically-elected policymakers care more about aggregate economic welfare and may see foreign ownership liberalization as a way to create new jobs, encourage transfer of more efficient technologies, and improve payment imbalances by raising exports. As I discuss in Chapter 3, these benefits to FDI are less likely in the presence of ownership restrictions. Restrictions deter the investments that are most likely to generate these positive spillovers.

More generally, democratization weakens vested interests and provides a window for new groups to emerge. Henisz and Zellner (2005) construct a norms-based framework in which institutional change creates a window during which there is support for overturning the status quo and attacking previously vested interests. Following democratization and economic liberalization, some industrial groups dissolved, because they could not survive without barriers to foreign competition and extensive government subsidies. Guillén (2000a) identified several Spanish conglomerates that folded after democratization and economic reform. Other industrial groups became advocates for political change when autocratic leaders became less capable of delivering generous subsidies. For example, in Mexico in the 1980s, a growing segment of industrial interests grew weary of economic policies that put a drain on overall economic growth. They shifted their support away from the dominant party, the PRI, to the emerging PAN party.

Democratization increases the size of both the electorate and the winning coalition, requiring politicians to gain the support of more individuals than were necessary under autocratic rule. Studies of trade policy show that politicians place lower weight on the preferences of specialized interests as countries democratize (Mitra, Thomakos, and Ulubaşoğlu 2002, Milner and Kubota 2005, Milner and Mukherjee 2009).[41] Similarly countries liberalize their capital accounts following democratization (Quinn and Inclan 1997, Eichengreen and Leblang 2008).

2.5 Sources of Cross-Industry Variation: Organization of Production

The specific factors model implies that returns to domestic firms decline following the entry of an MNC affiliate. Local firms' productivity declines because of higher product costs owing to rising wages. Those firms in industries that receive market-oriented FDI also face product market competition

---

[41] Kono (2006) argues that democratization prompts a switch to less transparent forms of trade barriers. I empirically test this argument in Chapter 5.

from more productive firms whose products are often of higher quality and lower cost than were produced locally. Indeed, firm-level studies confirm that FDI inflows reduce the net productivity of domestic firms in the same industry (Aitken, Harrison, and Lipsey 1996, Sembenelli and Siotis 2008, Balsvik and Haller 2011) and compete away product market rents (Blonigen, Tomlin, and Wilson 2004, Chari and Gupta 2008).

The model identifies a source of variation in FDI's distributive costs across industries. All FDI inflows raise domestic firms' labor costs by increasing domestic labor demand. Market-oriented FDI also increases product market competition, captured by the model as a decline in the market price for an industry's market commodity in addition to the increase in the supply of industry-specific capital. This implies that firms exposed to market-oriented FDI tend to face greater losses relative to firms exposed to export-oriented FDI. Accordingly, industries into which market-oriented investment dominates are more likely to be regulated than industries with greater export-oriented FDI. This claim follows directly from the theory but I draw on empirical findings to flesh out additional aspects of industries that systematically influence local firms' exposure to FDI-induced product market competition.

Over time a greater proportion of total FDI was oriented toward exports as MNCs developed production networks spanning multiple countries. This shift reflected the rapidly declining costs of such production, including a decline in trade barriers and communications costs. Trade costs, particularly trade barriers, made the cost of export-oriented strategies too high. Production inputs could be subject to import duties. With the growth of export-oriented investments there was less demand for protection in those industries in which FDI did not create product market competition.

In Chapter 6 I test the implications of this claim for cross-industry patterns in foreign-ownership regulations. I estimate a industry-level count model of the number of countries that limit foreign ownership in each industry in 2000. With this empirical specification, I correlate industry characteristics with how often countries restrict FDI inflows into that industry. This analysis shows that more countries restrict ownership into industries that receive higher proportions of market-oriented FDI inflows as opposed to industries in which FDI tends to be export-oriented. Firms in the former type of industry have, all else equal, a greater incentive to lobby for ownership regulations to insulate against MNC competition.

As noted in the previous chapter, export-oriented FDI is more common in manufacturing industries whereas market-oriented FDI frequently flows into services. Most services cannot be traded at arm's length and only recently have such markets emerged so market-oriented FDI into these industries is one of the few conduits through which they are exposed to international competition. This distinction explains why, in a given cross-section, countries more frequently restrict FDI into service industries than into manufacturing and why this disparity has grown over time.

Implicit in this claim is the assumption that industries that face higher costs from FDI inflows have a greater incentive to lobby for restrictions and/or are more successful in securing them (Brock and Magee 1978, Irwin 1994,1996). Trade policy scholars have argued that although monopolistically competitive industries face a lower expected cost to trade competition they have more incentives to lobby for protection because lobbying is a private good (Gilligan 1997, Kono 2008). In order to interpret my findings as evidence of variation in distributive consequences, I must control for industry characteristics that influence local firms' propensity to lobby for restrictions. The empirical model in Chapter 6 includes controls for industry concentration, a common metric of an industry's collection action costs, and for the extent to which an industry is monopolistically competitive. One of the counterarguments I noted above is that monopolistic competition lowers the costs of new product market competition. The empirical estimate for this control variable indicates the net effect of these two opposing consequences of market structure for the incidence of regulation.

The second counterargument is that local firms prefer unrestricted FDI inflows because they anticipate productivity spillovers. To the extent that such spillovers do occur they emerge after substantial restructuring of industries including new investments by local firms to remain competitive. This pattern is very close to that observed among domestic firms following trade liberalization. The initial shock of foreign competition raises industry productivity by pushing the least productive firms out of the market and encouraging remaining domestic firms to pursue productivity enhancements to remain competitive (Pavcnik 2002, Melitz 2003, Tybout 2003, Bustos 2011). The ultimate productivity increases do not occur because of initial passive receipt of technology spillovers but rather aggressive efforts by domestic firms to remain competitive following entry of an MNC into their market and the exit of the least productive among domestic firms in the industry. These efforts are also necessary to absorb possible spillovers from MNC affiliates. For example, longer-term productivity increases are observed in only those industries with high levels of research and development spending, a proxy for firms' ability to capture possible spillovers from MNCs (Sembenelli and Siotis 2008, Keller and Yeaple 2009). The empirical model in Chapter 6 controls for average firm research spending in an industry to proxy for potential spillovers.

2.6 Conclusion

This chapter lays the foundations for a political economy theory of FDI regulation. It explained why firms would choose to become multinational and which firms actually do so. MNCs choose FDI primarily to produce and/or sell goods in foreign markets while maintaining control over their productive assets. These fundamentals of FDI are necessary to specify what economic activities MNCs engage in and how they compare to local firms in the countries in which they invest. The ways in which firms organize their investments across countries provides another analytical building block by indicating the range of activities that MNCs undertake in host countries. The organization of production is important to understanding why countries shift toward liberalization over time, because it links larger shifts in the world economy to the change in the content of FDI's distributive effects.

In the second half of the chapter I present a theoretical model of FDI's distributive effects, how it redistributes income among economic actors in recipient countries. Key model assumptions derive from the material presented in this chapter. I treat FDI as the inflow of specific capital that is more productive than existing specific capital in the recipient country. This assumption is based on the stylized facts presented in this chapter – that FDI is firm-specific capital and that only the world's most productive firms undertake FDI because of its high fixed costs. The distinction between export- and market-oriented FDI is a source of variation in FDI's distributive effects; only market-oriented FDI introduces product market competition. The consequence of formal ownership restrictions – sharing technology and revenues with local partners – explains why local capital owners prefer FDI regulation to unrestricted FDI inflows. In short, the nuances of FDI are indispensible to deriving its distributive effects.

Chapter 3 builds directly on the concepts presented here by opening up discussion of the policy instruments that countries use to regulate FDI inflows, the consequences of these policies, and regulation's effects on the quality and quantity of FDI that countries receive. Countries regulate FDI inflows in hopes of *weakening multinational firms' control over their own firm-specific assets*. More precisely FDI restrictions require MNCs to share their technologies and/or the income that they generate as a condition of entering the market. These regulations take the form of entry barriers that stipulate FDI must occur through joint ventures with local firms or policies regarding MNCs' production practices that have a similar effect of funneling technology and income to locals.

Chapter 3 describes the policy instruments that countries use to regulate FDI. I introduce the original measure of foreign ownership restrictions that I analyze in Chapters 5 and 6 to test my claims about the sources of cross-national and cross-industry variation. I explain how ownership restrictions blunt the distributive effects of unfettered FDI inflows and the larger economic policy context in which the policies emerged. The chapter closes with a brief empirical analysis of FDI inflows that demonstrates that countries with more extensive foreign ownership regulations receive less FDI on average.

3

FDI Regulation Weakens Control over Assets

FDI is a way for firms to expand internationally while maintaining control over their firm-specific assets. By restricting FDI, countries weaken MNC control over their productive assets by requiring MNCs to share their assets with local firms as a condition of entry or by otherwise limiting how MNCs deploy their assets. This motive is distinct from a simple desire to protect local producers from competition or raise revenue in the manner of a tariff or capital control. This chapter describes specific ways that countries regulate FDI, with an emphasis on foreign-ownership restrictions, the most common and broadly applicable form of FDI regulation. This chapter also shows how foreign-ownership restrictions mitigate FDI's distributive consequences by channelling firm-specific assets to local firms. A statistical analysis confirms that countries with higher average foreign ownership regulations tend to receive less FDI.

3.1 Instruments of FDI Regulation

FDI regulations are by and large national economic policies.[1] Efforts at international cooperation on FDI liberalization have yielded mixed results. In 1997, the Organization for Economic Cooperation and Development proposed the Multilateral Agreement on Investment, a treaty that would

---

[1] Local and regional policies also have bearing on FDI inflows. There are examples of local municipalities that regulate the entry of foreign-owned firms into the provision of basic public services like water, power, and sewage. Typically, however, subnational policymakers are more active in policies that attract investment rather than limit it. Often there is competition among subnational units to attract investors to one jurisdiction over another. Some countries grant subnational policymakers wide latitude in this regard. For instance, China, starting in the 1980s, devolved much of its FDI regulation to provinces and localities that in turn leveraged it into more investment through lax regulation (Huang 2003).

have required countries to phase out national FDI regulations. The proposal drew the ire of civil society groups concerned about FDI's consequences for human rights, labor standards, and the environment. A year later, the OECD abandoned the proposal in response to these protests. Two World Trade Organization (WTO) agreements deal with FDI regulation. The 1995 Agreement on Trade-Related Investment Measures bans the use of performance requirements as indirect trade barriers. The 1995 General Agreement on Trade in Services allows countries to make voluntary commitments to liberalize foreign ownership in services sectors like telecommunications and finance.

Since the late 1990s, preferential trade agreements increasingly have investment liberalization provisions that extend the concept of most-favored-nation (MFN) status to the FDI context. For example, Chapter 11 of the North American Free Trade Agreement (NAFTA) requires member countries to extend most-favored-nation status to firms based in other NAFTA countries, a standard that ensures firms access at least as open as the country grants to firms from any other country in the world. Bilateral investment treaties (BITs) have limited implications for FDI restrictions. These treaties emphasize dispute settlement procedures and tax harmonization rather than market access issues. Countries may codify existing national regulations into the treaties, but they typically do not address market access. FDI commitments embedded in trade agreements and the popularity of BITs arose *after* worldwide FDI restrictions declined; therefore they did not initiate FDI liberalization.

The precise legal form of regulations varies widely, ranging from administrative regulations to national laws and even constitutional prohibitions on foreign ownership. By all indications, governments enforce FDI regulations consistently.[2] Sometimes countries exempt firms that introduce new technology or otherwise fulfill some economic need. Some countries have relaxed investment rules temporarily in response to changing macroeconomic needs for FDI such as payment imbalances (Haggard 1990). Other countries extend investment incentives to encourage certain types of technology transfer; criteria are public information, and all foreign-owned firms are eligible. MNCs may engage in corruption to circumvent FDI regulations, but research shows that corruption deters FDI, especially

---

[2]   In general countries establish a single set of FDI regulations that apply to firms from all foreign countries. Regulations themselves do not discriminate between sending countries, but in practice host countries can discriminate informally. For example, many former Soviet Republics make it more difficult for Russian firms to invest than they do for West European MNCs.

by technologically advanced firms.[3] Even if countries do not consistently enforce regulations, uncertainty regarding their enforcement is likely to deter MNCs from investing.[4] To support this conclusion, I show later in this chapter that countries with informal barriers to investment receive lower volumes of FDI inflows.

There are two classes of regulatory instruments: entry restrictions and post-entry regulations unique to MNCs (i.e. regulations to which otherwise identical domestic firms are not subject). I focus my empirical analysis on entry restrictions. Formal entry barriers have several virtues as a proxy for formal FDI regulation. They are clear and transparent barriers that can be readily compared across countries and industries. They broadly apply to all industries as opposed to other types of restrictions that target advanced manufacturing industries. By contrast, many instruments of post-entry regulation are relevant for only some industries. For example, requirements that MNCs source a set percent of their production inputs locally are meaningful only for advanced manufacturing. I describe the full range of regulatory instruments in the Appendix.

My primary measure of FDI regulation is restrictions on foreign ownership.[5] These are limits on the equity share that foreign firms may own in a single company. Because of ownership restrictions, MNCs must form joint ventures with local firms. Joint ventures are collaborations that can span multiple parts of the production process including research, production, and distribution. Foreign-ownership limits achieve the goal of technology transfer through these mandatory joint ventures. I describe the mechanics of this process below.[6] Countries usually set ownership restrictions at the industry level. The unit of observation in the raw data is country-industry-

[3] Javorcik and Wei (2000). Although studies examine general corruption levels they suggest that corruption in the enforcement of FDI regulations deters FDI independent of the evaded regulation. Additionally, a growing number of countries prosecute MNCs based in their countries for corrupt practices abroad. U.S.-based MNCs have been subject to prosecution since the 1977 Foreign Corrupt Practices Act. Criminal liability in the home country makes MNCs less likely to evade FDI regulations through corruption.
[4] An analogy to trade is instructive. Countries impose tariff barriers on the entry of foreign goods, but customs enforcement may be inconsistent or importers can pay bribes in lieu of tariff duties. The uncertainty surrounding the true tariff cost is likely to deter some producers from exporting their goods to the market. Uncertainty regarding customs enforcement does not prevent trade scholars from treating tariff barriers as reliable metrics of trade restrictions.
[5] There are many informal and indirect ways that countries can de facto restrict FDI. Countries may prefer these strategies when they want to apply restrictions selectively. It is, however, difficult to identify the intended purpose of indirect policy measures. I discuss these issues and other aspects of FDI regulations in greater depth in the appendix.
[6] Occasionally countries ban foreign ownership completely.

year. For each observation I record the presence of a majority local ownership requirement. The binary coding is appropriate, because ownership limits almost always cap foreign ownership at 49 percent in order to prevent a foreigner from acquiring majority ownership of firms.

The data appendix to this book describes data sources and the data-collection process in depth. Here I briefly describe the choice of data sources and the country and industry scope of the data set. Regulatory data on other forms of international economic flows like tariff rates and capital controls are more readily available, because countries belong to multinational organizations that coordinate policies in these areas such as the WTO (tariffs) and the International Monetary Fund (IMF) (capital controls). These organizations require their members to regularly report their policies as part of their monitoring functions. No analogous organization exists to govern FDI, thus the absence of established data sources.

Two U.S. government publications are the sources for these data: *Overseas Business Reports* and *National Trade Barrier Estimates*. The former is a publication of the U.S. Commerce Department that describes countries' investment regulations, among other economic characteristics, as a service to the U.S. business community, and the latter is an annual report to the U.S. Congress of foreign countries' trade and investment barriers. These publications provide one of the few data sources on countries' FDI policies with extensive historical coverage.

The dataset covers approximately one hundred countries, all the countries for which data were available in the above-mentioned sources. As the United States is the world's largest source of FDI, it is reasonable to assume that the countries for which it provides commercial guidance encompass all salient or potentially salient destinations for U.S. investors. The dataset spans the range of advanced industrialized countries to small developing countries.[7] Not in the sample are the former communist countries of Eastern Europe and the Soviet Union, because data for those countries were available only for the last few years of the sample.[8]

The dataset covers industries that I hand-coded according to the International Standard Industrial Classification (ISIC) Revision 3, the

---

[7] Blonigen and Wang (2004) have argued against pooling industrialized and developing countries in analyses of FDI determinants and FDI's effects on growth because of different mechanisms at work in each set of countries. This is not a concern for models of FDI regulation because the consequences of inflows are not sensitive to the distinctions that they highlight.

[8] See Dorobantu (2011) for an analogous study of FDI liberalization in transition economies with results consistent with those presented in Chapter 5.

international classification scheme for all forms of productive activities, based on how the data sources described the industries. Although the data source typically indicated which industries had restrictions, it did not systematically discuss all industries in a country. Accordingly, I assume that all industries not specifically indicated as restricted had no foreign-ownership barriers.

From the raw data, I constructed a measure of foreign-ownership restrictions that captures the extent of restrictions for a country-year. *Entry Restriction* is the percent of all industries in a country-year in which foreign ownership is restricted. Most investment laws specify that foreign-owned firms are limited to a minority share of ownership; in practice this means 49 percent or less. I calculated this variable from the country-industry data on foreign ownership restrictions described above.[9] This measure could underestimate the true level of restriction because not all industries exist in all countries (e.g. the denominator may be too large).[10] This is most likely to be true of manufacturing industries because countries can import goods that are not produced domestically. I addressed this source of downward bias by using industry-level manufacturing data from the UN Industrial Development Organization to remove "null industries," industries that do not exist, as indicated by no employment or output in a given country-year.[11] Comparable data on service industries do not exist for this timeframe and country sample, so I assume that all service industries exist in all countries. This is more likely to be true in services than in manufacturing – most services cannot be imported – but it likely overestimates the number of service industries, and therefore probably underestimates the true extent of restrictions in an economy. I exclude primary sectors – agriculture, forestry, and mining – from my analysis. Due to the unique features of FDI into the primary sector – it has exceptionally large economies of scale and is very capital intensive – the distributional implications presented here are less likely to hold.

A less transparent form of entry barrier is a requirement that proposed investments undergo screening for potential threats to national interests. Countries vary in how they define national interest. Some have narrowly

---

[9] These are data measured at the most disaggregated industry level of the ISIC Rev 3, typically the four digit industry classification.

[10] Ideally these data would be weighted by the importance of each industry to the overall economy. Unfortunately the necessary disaggregated data on industry output or employment as a percent of GDP are unavailable for manufacturing and service industries. Such weighting schemes are also susceptible to bias because any meaningful weight is sure to be influenced by the presence of a restriction.

[11] UNIDO data are organized by ISIC Rev 2 classification so only industries that remain whole across the ISIC Rev 2-ISIC Rev 3 concordance are removed.

tailored screening criteria focused on national security.[12] For example, since 1991 all proposed foreign acquisitions of U.S. firms are subject to review by the Committee on Foreign Investment in the United States (CFIUS). CFIUS is a federal interagency panel with the authority to block acquisitions it deems harmful to U.S. national security. Other countries construe national interest broadly to include economic concerns like potential competition for local firms. In 2005, U.S. food conglomerate PepsiCo was rumored to have plans for a hostile takeover of Danone, the French producer of yogurt and bottled water. Amid sharp protests from French firms and politicians, the country's prime minister, Dominique de Villepin, pledged to block the takeover to "defend France's interests." De Villepin justified his threats by the assertion that Danone was strategically important to the French economy.[13] Governments can use screening requirements to selectively exclude foreign firms that pose a threat to salient domestic interests. Even when countries do not design screening procedures to be a substantial barrier to FDI, such procedures can create uncertainty and delays.

Investment Screening measures the percent of industries with informal regulatory requirements for a country-year. This measure captures the scope for unobservable, informal barriers to market entry. With these data I can test whether countries shift between formal and informal regulations. It is constructed in the same manner as *Entry Restriction*. Figure 3.1 compares average formal ownership restrictions to informal screening requirements. In most years screening requirements are more common than formal ownership restrictions but follow the same downward trend over time.

These two measures of FDI regulations appear in two sets of empirical models in this book. Later in this chapter I estimate models of the volume of FDI that countries receive. In Chapter 5 I model the liberalization of these restrictions over time as a function of countries' economic and political characteristics. The juxtaposition of formal and informal entry restrictions highlights three dimensions of my argument. First, in this chapter, I show that both formal and informal policies deter FDI inflows. This finding supports my earlier claim that restrictions deter FDI even if countries do not consistently enforce formal policies. Any uncertainty regarding enforcement closely approximates the uncertainty of the discretionary

---

[12] Some countries have voluntary screening to determine eligibility for investment incentives. Voluntary screening requirements are not included in this measure. The measure also omits routine registration requirements that do not include discretion over the terms of firm entry.

[13] "France flouts the Pepsi Challenge," *The Telegraph*, July 24, 2005.

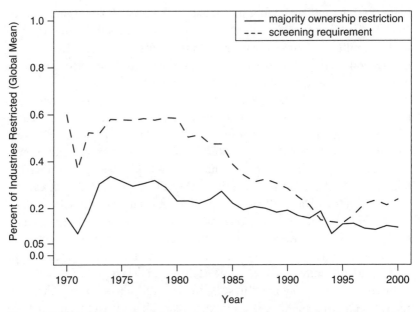

Figure 3.1 Global average foreign-ownership restrictions, formal versus informal barriers, 1970–2000.
Note: Figure plots formal entry restrictions (*Entry Restrictions*) and informal entry barriers (*Investment Screening*). See this chapter for variable descriptions.

screening process. Second, the distinction between formal and informal
distinction matters if countries that eliminate formal restrictions replace
them with informal barriers (Kono 2006). In Chapter 5, I show that democracies have lower levels of formal regulation but there is no systematic correlation between regime type and the informal FDI entry barriers. Third,
in Chapter 6 the distinction is relevant to parsing industry demand for formal regulation, a form of public good, and informal regulations that make
lobbying for FDI protection a private good by facilitating targeted, firm-
specific FDI barriers.

3.2 Why Local Capital Owners Profit from Restrictions on Foreign Ownership

Foreign-ownership restrictions force MNCs to enter into joint ventures
with local firms as a condition to entering the market. Normally firms vol-
untarily enter into joint ventures to exploit synergies between them for their
mutual gain. These ventures often involve joint research and development

projects, or marketing and distribution partnerships that capitalize on each participant's comparative advantage. For example, in 1984 General Motors and Toyota opened a joint automobile production plant in Fremont, California to produce cars for sale under their respective brands. The joint venture, New United Motor Manufacturing Inc. (NUMMI), gave General Motors hands-on experience with more efficient Japanese production practices and furnished Toyota with its first North American manufacturing facility staffed by unionized workers. Voluntary cross-border joint ventures such as NUMMI are common when the local partner can provide MNCs with location-specific advantages like local market expertise and access to product distribution channels. Some scholars of corporate strategy advocate joint ventures as an optimal mode of entry for developed country firms investing in developing economies because of the unique difficulties of operating in a developing economy.[14]

Joint ventures carry risks similar to licensing because partners have access to intangible, firm-specific assets. Even in voluntary joint ventures, participants confront risks to their control over firm-specific assets. In practice these concerns are not a significant barrier to voluntary joint ventures because all parties to the venture have specific assets, and the reciprocal nature of the incomplete contracting problem is sufficient motivation for the parties to respect each other's property rights (Oxley 1997).

When foreign-ownership restrictions effectively force MNCs to partner with local firms they are less likely to find partners with whom synergies arise organically even if they would have sought partnerships organically in the absence of restrictions. In some countries, like South Korea, MNCs were assigned partners by local government. Unlike voluntary joint ventures, these partnerships lack the incentive-based protections against asset expropriation by the local partner.

Ownership restrictions, via these forced joint ventures, reallocate income from MNCs to local firms by forcing MNCs to share productive assets with their local partners. Involuntary joint ventures pose a higher risk to MNCs' intangible assets than voluntary joint ventures because local partners have an incentive to appropriate the MNCs' assets. Unlike voluntary partnerships the local firms typically do not have assets of their own to incentivize respect for MNCs' property rights. In mandatory joint ventures, local firms receive access to more efficient production technologies and processes that are not available through other channels. Even if such

---

[14] Beamish and Banks (1987). Much of the evidence on the profitability of joint ventures face severe selection problems that make causal inference difficult.

technologies were available on the open market, the partnerships provide opportunities for the close observation and hands-on training necessary for local firms to gain a working command of the technology independent of the MNC. Beyond the specific assets that the local partners receive, firms gain invaluable training in general skills of entrepreneurship and management. Amsden and Hinkino (1994) assign foreign-technology acquisition a central role in the growth and success of firms in late developing countries. They write, "The capability to acquire foreign technology is transformed into organizational know-how that provides a key resource in the effectiveness of corporate growth through diversification" (112). Local firms accrue additional benefits from their alliance with MNCs including easier access to financing through MNCs' own internal capital markets and greater credibility with third-party lenders created by association with a multinational firm (Antràs, Desai, and Foley 2009).

Over the long term, ownership restrictions can be the first step in more direct expropriation of MNC assets or the income that they generate. Henisz (2002) identifies "contractual hazards" to joint ventures in which a local partner can use leverage vis-à-vis the host government to lobby for regulation that benefits the local firm at the expense of its multinational partner. MNCs balance predatory behavior from partners and host governments. Indeed, Henisz and Williamson (2000) suggest that local partners "may opportunistically approach the government with requests to take actions that have the effect of favoring them at the expense of the multinational" (267). Bradley (1977) showed that expropriation in joint ventures involving a foreign-owned partner was eight times more likely than expropriation in a joint venture between two domestic firms. Thus, ownership restrictions are a channel through which foreign firms are subject to risk.

Many of the countries that employed ownership restrictions did so in tandem with incentives designed to compensate for the costs of mandatory joint ventures. Countries appreciated that ownership restrictions would deter MNC investments so they sought to compensate by lowering the MNCs' production costs. Specific measures included land grants, subsidized inputs like electricity and other infrastructure, and exemption from tariffs on imported production inputs. Special economic zones (SEZs) are often mentioned in this regard but they hosted relatively little FDI. Between 1966 and 1970, only 23 percent of all FDI into Taiwan was based in an SEZ, and in subsequent years the percentages dropped (Haggard 1990, 201). SEZs in South Korea followed a similar pattern. In fact, the zones housed many domestic firms who manufactured on contract from foreign firms rather than MNC affiliates. Figures for MNCs' exports out of these countries are similarly low. At their peak during the period of active export promotion, MNCs' share of total exports in Taiwan and South Korea was approximately 30 percent, lower than both Brazil and Mexico. In 1975 only 14 percent of South Korean chemical exports were from Korean subsidiaries of MNCs (Haggard and Cheng 1987).

More generally, countries coupled investment incentives with ownership restrictions to serve the interests of local capital owners. Many mistake investment incentives as evidence of FDI liberalization, because these policies, when considered in isolation, ostensibly reveal an interest in attracting FDI. In the 1960s, South Korea placed no restrictions on foreign ownership in manufacturing. As domestic industrial capacity increased the country revised its investment laws in 1971 and 1973 to limit MNCs' market access. These revisions gave priority to investments with majority local ownership, severely limited the circumstances under which wholly foreign-owned firms could enter the market, and, at that, required an eventual transfer of ownership to a domestic firm. Rising wages in the 1970s spurred additional efforts to diversify the economy.[15] Countries stepped up their targeted efforts to attract investments in the right industries.

In most countries, the ownership of firms is relatively concentrated (La Porta, Lopez de Silanes, and Schliefer 1998).[16] Industrial groups, also called business groups or conglomerates, "typically consist of legally independent firms, operating in multiple (often unrelated) industries, which are bound together by persistent formal (e.g., equity) and informal (e.g., family) ties" (Khanna and Yefeh 2007, 331).[17] Ownership is concentrated within each firm and across the different firms within the group. The archetype of a

---

[15] Another distinctive feature of incentives in this period is that they were granted subject to several conditions that required recipient firms to transfer a minimum amount of technology or were limited to investments into high technology industries where the need for foreign capital was especially great.

[16] Concentration is present on two dimensions. Within a single firm, concentration refers to the distribution of ownership across investors. Ownership is diffuse when there are several equity investors. The archetype of diffuse ownership is a publically traded firm run by professional managers who are accountable to shareholders. Ownership is concentrated within a firm when one party is a majority owner and managers are de facto accountable to this one party. Concentration of ownership also describes the distribution of productive assets across the economy. On this dimension, ownership is concentrated when a few entities – firms or individuals – control a disproportionate share of assets across industries.

[17] Identifying industrial groups using this definition is sometimes a difficult task because key defining features, like the importance of informal ties, are not readily observable. More precise definitions rely on measures of diversification across linked firms and the integration of production between firms, but they do confirm the robustness of this stylized definition.

business group is a set of firms all owned and managed by members of a single family.

This industrial structure dampens incentives for innovation. Innovation is simply the creation of new firm-specific assets. Groups generate cash flow but they have little incentive to invest in innovation because they do not face competition. They are large enough to deter entry by other firms, especially in industries marked by high-scale economies. In most countries groups enjoyed the protection of import barriers (Guillén 2000b). The emergence of corporate research and development is spurred by market competition.[18] The concentration of wealth within these groups curbs innovation across the economy because there is insufficient capital to fund it.

Restrictions on foreign ownership provides the productive assets for groups to expand into unrelated industries. Groups not only acquire specific production technologies in the manner described but they also learn from foreign partners general skills of entrepreneurship and management and cultivate an internal pool of managerial talent. Expansion into unrelated sectors was only possible through technology obtained elsewhere and where firms learned the process of entering a new industry.[19] Guillén (2000b, 365) describes this capability as "a bundle of skills that facilitate conducting feasibility studies, obtaining licenses from the state, arranging financial packages, securing technology and knowhow, setting up plants, hiring and training workforces, and establishing supply and distribution channels." Ownership restrictions have the obvious added benefit of preventing market competition from more advanced foreign-owned firms. Perez Compac, Argentina's second-largest industrial group, expanded under the protection of foreign-ownership laws. Between 1973 and 1983, the group grew from ten firms to fifty-three firms in a wide range of industries (Guillén 2000b). There is also growing evidence that local partners in joint ventures are able to expropriate a proportionally higher share of returns.[20]

---

[18] Larger developing countries invested in a public research infrastructure to compensate for the lack of private innovation, but they were the exceptions rather than the rules. See Adler 1986 on Brazil and Grieco 1982 on India.

[19] The innovation process of late industrializers was different from countries that industrialized in the nineteenth century. In that earlier period, firms diversified through movement into related industries. These moves involved adapting existing technology for a new purpose. For example, DuPont, the U.S. chemicals firms, expanded from its initial specialty of chemicals used in explosives into related products including paints, dyes, and photographic film. The experience of late developers is different in that there was expansion into unrelated industries.

[20] Bertrand, Mehta, and Mullainathan (2002) suggest that majority owners expropriate the non-operation portion of profits out of the firm. This segment of business allows local firms to capitalize on information asymmetries vis-à-vis foreign investors.

3.3 Ownership Regulations Reduce FDI Inflows

Do foreign ownership regulations actually reduce FDI inflows? Given the asset internalization motives behind FDI, ownership restrictions should, all else equal, reduce FDI inflows. MNCs weigh the expected returns on investment against the costs of diminished control, including degradation of their assets and loss of associated income streams. The few existing studies of FDI regulation confirm this hypothesis for various small samples of country-years (Gomes-Casseres 1990, Wei 2000, Nicoletti et al. 2003).

With my country-level measure of FDI regulations, I can analyze how regulation affects volumes of FDI inflows on a larger scale than ever before. I measure the dependent variable, the volume of investment in a country-year with data from the External Wealth of Nations II database (Lane and Milesi-Ferretti 2007). Although aggregate FDI flow data have well-known inaccuracies, the estimates in this database have been adjusted for different methods of valuation and exchange-rate movements. From these data, I measure the volume of FDI in two ways. One measure is the ratio of FDI stock to total GDP, *FDI Stock/GDP*. This measure scales the value of FDI by the value of all economic activity in the economy. It is the most common measure of FDI volumes used in political economy research on FDI (Jensen 2006, Li and Resnick 2003). This measure, however, cannot differentiate between countries that receive low volumes of FDI and those that receive high volumes in absolute terms but have even greater volumes of economic activity. For this reason I generate a second measure of absolute FDI volume as the natural log of the total stock of FDI (the numerator of the other volume measure), *ln(FDI Stock)*. The logged value of FDI stock ensures that country-year outliers do not skew model estimates.

I measure ownership restrictions with the formal and informal measures of restrictions described in the previous section, *Entry Restrictions* and *Investment Screening*. Countries with higher values of these variables are expected to receive lower FDI volumes. Four host-country characteristics provide controls for common determinants of the amount of FDI that a country receives: GDP per capita, trade as a percentage of GDP, the presence of a currency crisis in the previous year, and natural resources as a percent of GDP. *Per capita GDP* captures the attractiveness of a market to an MNC. MNCs are more likely to invest in countries with higher incomes. They are especially likely to make market-oriented investments in wealthier countries because these countries have larger markets that can support larger scale production. *Trade/GDP*, the sum of exports and imports divided by GDP, indicates the country's openness to trade in a given year.

This measure captures the revealed level of trade in the economy. FDI and trade can be both substitutes and complements so the expected sign of this variable is not clear. Trade restrictions are a motivation for market-oriented FDI, but low trade barriers make export-oriented FDI more likely. *Currency Crisis* controls for the stimulating effect of currency crisis on FDI. Currency devaluation lowers the real costs of FDI and, all else equal, prompts greater investment (Froot and Stein 1991). *Primary Exports/GDP* controls for the effect of primary resources on FDI inflows. Countries abundant in natural resources are likely to receive FDI inflows independent of regulations. Control over resources gives countries unique leverage vis-à-vis MNCs. Although the measure of foreign ownership restrictions omits restrictions in primary sector industries, the presence of natural resources nonetheless influences the total volume of FDI that a country receives. A priori there is not a clear expectation about the sign of this coefficient; resource seeking FDI may increase total FDI inflows, but factors correlated with the presence of primary resources may make FDI into other sectors less attractive.

These data span up to 76 countries from 1970–2000. These data have a time-series cross-sectional structure in which the number of cross-sectional units exceeds the number of temporal intervals. In all likelihood these data violate multiple Ordinary Least Squares (OLS) assumptions. Under these conditions estimates of a naïve OLS model would produce incorrect standard errors. Following Beck and Katz (1995), I estimate OLS models with panel-corrected standard errors to account for contemporaneous correlation and panel heteroskedasticity. A panel-specific AR(1) correction addresses any serial correlation across error terms. I include country fixed effects to control for time invariant country characteristics and focus on sources of temporal variation within countries.[21] All explanatory variables are lagged by one year.[22] Table 3.1 provides summary statistics for all of the variables used in the analysis, and Table 3.2 provides the definitions and sources for all the data.

Table 3.3 presents estimates of four models. The first two models measure FDI volume as the ratio of FDI stock to GDP. In both models, FDI regulations have a statistically significant, inverse correlation with FDI

---

[21] Controls for time obscure substantively meaningful change in slow moving covariates.
[22] An obvious concern is that ownership restrictions are endogenous to FDI stocks despite the use of lagged restrictions. The standard solution, an instrumental variable regression, requires an instrument for foreign ownership restrictions that is simultaneously correlated with restrictions and uncorrelated with the volume of FDI in a country. To the best of my knowledge, no such instrument exists.

Table 3.1 *Summary statistics*

	Obs	Mean	Std. dev.	Min	Max
FDI Stock/GDP	2744	0.1575202	0.3708892	0	16.4997
Ln(FDI stock)	2712	7.424149	2.191305	0.7884573	13.30007
Entry Restrictions	2255	0.1955825	0.3673188	0	1
Investment Screening	1525	0.3427363	0.4642883	0	1
Ln(per capita GDP)	2868	7.765666	1.390695	4.442014	10.80627
Trade/GDP	2843	0.6571892	0.4057205	0.0106414	2.908523
Primary Exports/GDP	2106	26.60666	31.12649	0.048622	100
Currency Crisis	2911	0.3668842	0.4820374	0	1

volume. Model 1 measures restrictions with the measure of formal ownership restrictions. Countries with restrictions that are one standard deviation above the mean receive approximately .2 percentage points less FDI than countries with restrictions equal to the sample mean. Countries with the mean level of entry barrier, approximately 19 percent of industries subject to entry barriers, have FDI inflows of over one percent of their GDP. The signs of the other statistically significant coefficients are consistent with basic models of FDI determinants. Countries with higher per capita GDP and trade flows receive higher volumes of FDI. Model 2 confirms the statistically significant and inverse correlation when volume is measured as the total stock of FDI.

Models 3 and 4 replace the measure of formal regulation with the measure of investment screening requirements. In both models, the coefficient on *Investment Screening* has the expected negative sign and is statistically significant. Countries with screening requirements equal to one standard deviation above the mean receive .04 percentage points less FDI than countries with requirements equal to the sample mean. This finding supports the claim that FDI regulations deter FDI even when there is a possibility that firms can evade the restriction. Screening requirements capture the uncertainties regarding regulation that deter MNCs from investing. As with the first pair of results, per capita GDP and trade have the expected positive and statistically significant coefficients. Model 4 confirms the results hold for a measure of absolute volume of FDI stock.

Still unanswered, however, is the question of why MNCs invest in a country with ownership restrictions. In some cases the expected returns on FDI outweigh the risks of a mandatory joint venture. These cases usually involve access to a specialized production input or a particularly attractive product market. Firm-level studies of FDI show that MNCs that invest in the

Table 3.2 *Data definitions and sources*

(units = country-year)

	Definition	Source
FDI/GDP	FDI Stock /GDP*	Calculated using data from External Wealth of Nations Database, Mark II (Lane and Milesi-Ferretti 2007).
Ln(FDI stock)	Natural log of FDI stock measured in constant U.S. dollars*	Calculated using data from External Wealth of Nations Database, Mark II (Lane and Milesi-Ferretti 2007).
Entry Restrictions	Percentage of industries with limits or complete bans on foreign-equity ownership	Original data as described in the text.
Investment Screening	Percentage of industries into which FDI is subject to a discretionary screening process	Original data as described in the text.
Ln (per capita GDP)	Natural log of per capita GDP (constant 2000 U.S. dollars)	World Development Indicators, World Bank
Trade/GDP	(Exports+imports)/GDP	World Development Indicators, World Bank
GDP Growth	Percentage growth in GDP	World Development Indicators, World Bank
Primary Exports/GDP	Primary exports/GDP	Sachs and Warner (1995)
Currency Crisis	= 1 if nominal exchange rate depreciates by at least 25% and exceeds the previous year's depreciation by at least 10%	Leblang and Satyanath (2008)

* *Note:* Measure employs the standard statistical definition of FDI as foreign-equity ownership in excess of ten percent.

presence of restrictions are relatively less efficient or are efficient firms that choose to transfer less efficient technologies than they would have otherwise. Only less efficient firms are willing to compromise control over their assets in order to gain access to a market. The generous subsidies offered by industrializing countries create incentives for less efficient firms to enter. Murtha (1991) argues that MNCs attracted by government incentives and

Table 3.3 *Determinants of FDI volume*

	(1)	(2)	(3)	(4)
	FDI stock/ GDP	Ln(FDI stock)	FDI stock/ GDP	Ln(FDI stock)
Entry Restrictions (t–1)	−0.00595+	−0.102**		
	(0.00351)	(0.0361)		
Investment Screening (t–1)			−0.00998**	−0.142**
			(0.00363)	(0.0328)
Ln(per capita GDP) (t–1)	0.0799**	2.321**	0.0559**	2.239**
	(0.0142)	(0.172)	(0.0151)	(0.178)
Trade/GDP (t–1)	0.0386+	−0.0193	0.0816**	0.783**
	(0.0213)	(0.205)	(0.0209)	(0.216)
Primary Exports/GDP (t–1)	−7.78e-05	−0.00270+	−0.000210	−0.00170
	(0.000168)	(0.00148)	(0.000146)	(0.00142)
Currency Crisis (t–1)	0.00176	0.00236	0.00113	0.0117
	(0.00215)	(0.0198)	(0.00218)	(0.0214)
Constant	−0.618	−11.44**	−0.408*	−10.81**
	(0.513)	(1.622)	(0.172)	(1.811)
Observations	1,375	1,373	1,111	1,109
N(Countries)	76	76	62	62

** $p < 0.01$, * $p < 0.05$, + $p < 0.1$
Note: Panel-corrected standard errors in parentheses. All models include country-fixed effects and a panel-specific AR(1) correction.

subsidies tend to be less efficient. They need subsidies in order for multi-national production to be efficient. Alternately, efficient firms may chose to transfer older, less productive technologies whose leakage would not compromise a critical firm asset.[23]

In addition, firms who invest because of artificially low labor costs are less likely to make long-term investments in training and infrastructure development because the risk that oppressive labor policies will end is high. To the extent that there are backward linkages from investment they are less likely to obtain when FDI occurs through joint ventures (Moran 1998). Thus, even when countries continue to receive FDI inflows in the presence of restrictions these investments are of a poorer quality. Restrictions will select for the less productive firms willing to invest under these circumstances or, alternately, firms will transfer less productive technologies to minimize the losses of forgoing control over productive assets.

[23] Stopford and Wells (1972), Svejnar and Smith (1984), Blomström and Sjöholm (1999).

Thus there are two clear implications to formal ownership regulations: a decline in FDI inflows and those investments that do occur are of poorer quality. Together, these effects establish the implications of foreign-ownership restrictions for MNCs' investment choices. They demonstrate that restrictions affect the decision to invest in a country and the specific content of that investment. It might be argued that countries are willing to negotiate with MNCs and that formal policy barriers are simply a starting point for those negotiations; countries negotiate less restrictive terms of entry with specific MNCs that they hope will invest. That may be true in some instances, but the mere presence of a restriction increases the costs associated with the investment due to the necessary negotiations. Additionally, it suggests a higher risk that special, one-off arrangements may be withdrawn given that there is a revealed policy preference for protection.

3.4 Conclusion

This chapter describes FDI regulations, the policies that countries use to weaken MNCs' control over their assets. Foreign ownership restrictions require MNCs to be minority shareholders in joint partnerships with local firms. Through these forced partnerships local firms gain access to MNCs' technologies and their associated income streams. These policies are one of the few conduits for firms in industrializing countries to access new technologies. After presenting a new measure of foreign ownership regulation I estimate a model of FDI inflows that includes this new measure as a parameter. Countries with more extensive foreign ownership regulations do in fact receive lower volumes of FDI inflows.

The following chapters turn to empirical tests of my claims. The detailed, firm-level dynamics that I describe should be kept in mind in the context of the more aggregate studies of policy outcomes. These microfoundations keep in perspective how individuals and firms are affected by broader changes in political regimes and the organization of economic activity. Chapter 4 considers the sources of individual-level FDI preferences. Chapters 5 and 6 both draw on the foreign-ownership restrictions data described here in order to test claims about cross-country and cross-industry sources of variation in the frequency of foreign-ownership regulations respectively.

4

Individual Preferences for FDI Inflows

In May 2006, Bolivian President Evo Morales nationalized his country's natural gas reserves in what was the first of several nationalizations of foreign-owned companies in the years that followed. Dispatching military troops to take possession of the companies' facilities, the president declared: "The time has come, the awaited day, a historic day in which Bolivia retakes absolute control of our natural resources. The looting by foreign companies has ended."[1] Morales's statement illustrates a common sentiment that citizens, especially those of less-developed countries, perceive FDI as exploitation. Such sentiments contrast sharply with pro-FDI policies of international investment agreements and generous FDI incentives.

This chapter analyzes the roots of public opinion regarding FDI inflows to shed new light on this puzzling contradiction. In Chapter 2 I provided the theoretical logic for how FDI inflows raise wages in recipient countries and summarized the considerable supporting evidence. At the same time, I acknowledged two economic consequences outside of the model's scope that could diminish labor's enthusiasm for FDI: increased volatility of labor demand and the introduction of labor-saving technologies. There may also be noneconomic drivers of labor FDI preferences, like the nationalism suggested in Morales's comments, that decrease the probability that labor supports FDI.

My hypotheses about the determinants of FDI regulation rest on claims about individual preferences for FDI, making this a particularly important puzzle to address. I argue that average levels of foreign-ownership regulation declined over the sample period because policy makers in democratized developing countries are more responsive to labor's economic policy preferences. In order to interpret the inverse correlation between democratization

[1] "History Helps to Explain Bolivia's New Boldness," *New York Times*, May 7, 2006.

and regulation as evidence of labor's political clout I need to confirm that, on average, labor supports FDI inflows. Such a confirmation requires parsing the various economic and noneconomic sources of preferences.

In this chapter I analyze 1990s public opinion data from seventeen Latin American countries to show that, indeed, labor supports FDI and that support is more likely among workers who anticipate the largest wages increases due to FDI inflows. Analysis of public opinion data provides a direct and novel means with which to test claims about individual policy preferences. Individual policy preferences can be directly linked to salient demographic information regarding education, employment, and social attitudes. By contrast, indirect measures of preferences based on political behavior are much noisier due to the influence of interest groups and political institutions on observed behavior (Rodrik 1995).

A growing body of political economy research takes this approach to test how consistent policy preferences are with anticipated distributive effects. Scholars have tested individual preferences for international economic flows like trade and immigration but not FDI.[2] Scheve and Slaughter (2004) show that British workers were less likely to express job security if employed in manufacturing industries with higher levels of FDI activity but the authors note the ways in which FDI can also increase labor welfare. Scheve and Slaughter conclude: "We regard this tension [between FDI's positive and negative consequences for labor] to be an important issue in any research attempting to explain the politics of foreign investment policies in advanced economies" (673). Existing research based on claims about FDI preferences does not grapple with these complexities.[3]

Survey data also provides rich information about each respondent that I use to test for noneconomic sources of FDI policy preferences. Surveys provide proxies for respondents' nationalism, and that permits consideration of how one's broad orientation toward international affairs shapes policy preferences or even trumps distributive concerns (Mansfield and Mutz 2009, Naoi and Kume 2011). Anti-FDI rhetoric often frames FDI as a neocolonial threat to national sovereignty and arguably is of a sharper tone than opposition to other forms of foreign economic flows. For example, in April 2012, Argentine president Cristina Fernandez de Kirchner nationalized the local affiliate of Spanish oil company Repsol, Argentina's largest

---

[2] Trade: Scheve and Slaughter (2001a), O'Rourke and Sinnott (2001), Mayda and Rodrik (2004), Hainmueller and Hiscox (2006), Mansfield and Mutz (2009). Immigration: Scheve and Slaughter (2001b), Hainmueller and Hiscox (2007, 2010).

[3] Pinto and Pinto (2008) attribute to political parties FDI preferences such that left parties are more favorable to FDI into industries that are labor complements.

company. She justified the act as a "recovery of sovereignty and the control of a fundamental instrument."[4]

This framing of FDI could recast individual perceptions of FDI from an issue of personal welfare maximization to one of national unity against a foreign threat (regardless of whether an objective threat exists). I demonstrate empirically that these sentiments do not systematically correlate with respondents' support for FDI by accounting for survey respondents' nationalist sentiment.[5]

The survey sample, Latin American countries in the 1990s, facilitates broader inferences about the micropolitics of FDI. Recall from Figure 1.3 that Latin American countries exhibited the most dramatic fluctuations in foreign ownership regulations of any region during the sample period. The experiences of Latin American countries are prominent examples of the larger economic and political trends that produced FDI liberalization. In the early part of the sample period almost all countries in the region embraced import substitution industrialization including tight controls on foreign ownership to facilitate the growth of local firms. Widespread democratization preceded the dismantling of these restrictions while the region became a hub for export-oriented investments. The survey data cover years in which countries actively grappled with the role of FDI in the context of extensive and often divisive economic reforms (Stokes 2001). This backdrop makes for particularly compelling tests of preferences because responses reflect the range of factors that contributed to greater FDI openness.[6]

4.1 Modeling Preferences: Comparing Economic and Noneconomic Factors

My central claim is that labor prefers unrestricted FDI inflows because MNCs' production activities raise labor demand in host countries. MNCs

---

[4] "Behind Argentine seizure, a complex tale," *Washington Post*, April 26, 2012.

[5] There is reason to doubt the widespread appeal of nationalist arguments against FDI. Nationalist opposition is typically aimed at a specific foreign country and, rather than formal legislation barring investment from those countries, informal barriers are used to deter and block such investments. Fayerweather (1982) finds the perceptions of foreign-owned firms vary with the nationality of the firm. Additionally, some industries are more likely to raise nationalist concerns than others. These facts suggest that countries are more likely to use informal barriers to deter specific investors rather than across-the-board limits on all FDI. Nationalist justifications can also mask rent-seeking policies. Breton's (1964) account of Quebecois nationalism demonstrates how nationalist claims are used instrumentally to reallocate wealth to particular groups.

[6] Analyses of earlier survey samples are consistent with the findings presented here. These surveys also include local firm owners and find that they consistently opposed unrestricted FDI (Sugges 1982 and Dominguez 1982).

have particularly high demand for skilled workers due to the technical sophistication of their productive assets. Accordingly, the more skilled respondents are, the more likely they are to support unrestricted FDI. This claim derives from the specific factors model of FDI's distributive effects presented in the previous chapter.

Preferences are, however, complex and multi-dimensional, and empirical tests must account for the diverse inputs to FDI preferences. As noted in Chapter 2, there are counterarguments for why labor might oppose FDI inflows. FDI might reduce net labor welfare if it makes jobs less secure by raising the volatility of labor demand. Similarly, if FDI introduces labor-saving technologies, it could reduce net labor demand. The previous chapter lists theoretical reasons and empirical evidence against these counterarguments, but I nonetheless include them here in my empirical analysis of preferences to further validate the specific factors model as an accurate representation of FDI's income effects. The nationalist salience attached to FDI via anti-FDI rhetoric might fuel labor opposition independent of anticipated income effects. Studies of trade policy preferences find that respondents who express greater national pride are less likely to support free trade.[7]

Assessing the role of skill variation in the probability of FDI support presents both theoretical and empirical challenges. There is a theoretical question of what constitutes skilled versus unskilled labor with specific regard to MNCs' labor demand and an empirical question of how to measure this variation in skill. Research on the labor market consequences of economic integration relies on the distinction between production and nonproduction workers to refer to unskilled and skilled workers respectively.

Production workers are "workers (up through the working foreman level) engaged in fabricating, processing, assembling, inspecting and other manufacturing." Nonproduction workers are "personnel, including those engaged in supervision (above the working foreman level), installation and servicing of own product, sales, delivery, professional, technological, administrative, etc." (Berman et al. 1994, 369)

The empirical research on FDI's wage effects that I discussed in Chapter 3 often employs this distinction. For instance, Feenstra and Hanson (1997) find that FDI into Mexico raised production wages but raised nonproduction wages even more. The related measurement issue is how to map survey respondents' known characteristics onto this theoretical distinction. I follow

---

[7] Mayda and Rodrik (2005), O'Rourke and Sinnott (2001).

the norm of survey-based studies of preferences in using respondents' education as an indicator of skill. It is not obvious what levels of educational attainment correspond to production and nonproduction employment in MNCs in 1990s Latin America. In particular, nonproduction work includes occupational activities that may correspond to a wide range of education levels or on-the-job training. The activities of many service sector MNCs fall outside of this standard definition

Considering the issue from a different perspective we might ask: how unskilled can an individual be and still anticipate higher wages from unrestricted FDI? The answer to this question establishes the lower bound for the likelihood of FDI support. Only if a majority supports FDI or is indifferent toward it can I plausibly argue in Chapter 5 that democratization generates FDI liberalization by raising the political influence of labor. My conservative answer to the question looks only at the prospects of direct employment by an MNC, setting aside the many indirect ways in which FDI could generate demand for low skilled labor (e.g. construction). The least skilled forms of MNC employment are in basic export-oriented product assembly. In Latin America these investments are often referred to as maquiladoras, factories concentrated close to national borders as part of multi-country supply chains. Alternately, the investments are located in officially designated export processing zones that are exempt from certain tariffs and regulations.[8] Although precise estimates of worker characteristics in the sector are scarce, surveys conducted in multiple countries place the average educational attainment of their workers at between six and eight years of formal schooling (Ver Beek 2001, Cling, Razafindrarakto, and Roubaud 2005). Accordingly, the probability of supporting unrestricted FDI inflows is likely higher among respondents with at least six years of formal schooling because empirically they occupy the lowest skilled jobs that MNCs create.

---

[8] These investments are technically FDI insofar as they are foreign-owned firms. However they lack many of the defining properties of FDI discussed in Chapter 2. Typically the foreign-owned firm is not internalizing highly productive assets in the manner of more sophisticated industries like automobiles or chemicals. Rather they produce on contract for unaffiliated companies. For example, a Taiwanese firm establishes a garment factory in Guatemala to produce apparel for U.S. firms. Technically this is FDI, and the Taiwanese firm has specialized assets in garment manufacturing but it is qualitatively different from scholarly definitions of FDI based on the internalization of assets. It is closer to a hybrid of FDI and outsourcing. For the purpose of pinning down labor support for FDI, however, it is appropriate to treat these investments as FDI because the average workers are likely to consider them as such.

Finally, my choice to measure skill by educational attainment is problematic if respondents' nationalist associations with FDI systematically correlate with their education level. Hainmueller and Hiscox (2006) propose that higher education uniquely socializes individuals to have more cosmopolitan preferences by fostering an awareness and appreciation of foreign cultures and influences. Higher education, they continue, also provides the requisite economic literacy to appreciate the welfare gains to free trade. These proposed effects of higher education on preferences are independent of the effect of higher education on returns to skills. To verify my central claim I must show empirically that support for FDI is not confined to university-educated respondents but that lesser-educated respondents who anticipate wage increases should also be more likely to support unrestricted FDI inflows.

4.2 Explaining FDI Preferences: Empirical Tests

Public opinion data are from the Latinobarometer, an annual public opinion survey conducted in seventeen Latin American countries.[9] This survey is unique among the prominent multi-country survey programs in that it regularly includes questions on attitudes toward FDI inflows. The surveys draw representative samples in each country and inquire about a wide range of political and social topics. Surveys from 1995, 1998, and 2001 included questions about FDI preferences. The 1995 and 1998 surveys ask:

Do you consider that foreign investment, in general, is beneficial or is it harmful to the economic development of the country?

Respondents replied "beneficial" or "harmful." [10] *FDI Beneficial* is a binary variable equal to 1 if the respondent answered "beneficial." The 1998 and 2001 surveys ask a different but related question:

Do you strongly agree, agree, disagree, or strongly disagree with the phrase: foreign investment should be encouraged?

---

[9] Latinobarometer Countries: Argentina, Bolivia, Brazil, Chile, Colombia, Costa Rica, Ecuador, El Salvador, Guatemala, Honduras, Mexico, Nicaragua, Panama, Paraguay, Peru, Uruguay, and Venezuela. The 1998 and 2001 surveys include all seventeen countries. Eight countries were in the 1995 survey: Argentina, Brazil, Chile, Mexico, Paraguay, Peru, Uruguay, and Venezuela.

[10] For all survey questions, nonresponses (e.g. "I do not know") are treated as missing values.

Promote FDI is equal to 1 if the respondent replied agree or strongly agree.[11] The use of two different questions, both of which are present in the 1998 sample, mitigates concerns about the effects of question wording by allowing comparisons across the two questions for the same sample.[12]

Labor's skill level is the central source for FDI preferences because of FDI's effect on returns to skills.[13] As is standard in empirical work on economic preferences I use respondents' level of education as a proxy for skill. There is, however, some disagreement over the most appropriate measure of educational attainment. Rather than choose among them, I utilize three distinct measures of education, each of which captures a somewhat different aspect of the same underlying concept. *Years of Education* measures the respondents' number of years of schooling (up to sixteen years).[14] This measure assumes a strictly linear effect of education on skill level. By construction each additional of year of education is assumed to have the same effect on the probability of FDI support. Scheve and Slaughter (2001b) measure educational attainment in this way. A different approach is to use the highest level of education completed as the proxy for skills. I construct two variables on this basis. *Education Level* is a four-category variable equal to 0 for less than a primary school education (including illiterate), 1 for completed primary school, 2 for completed secondary education, and 3 for completed higher education.[15] This measure collapses educational attainment into

[11] Results are unchanged using a four-category, ordered version of this variable. It might be argued that "foreign investment" refers to all forms of capital investment, not just FDI. This is unlikely given that the Spanish version of these questions refer to "la inversión extranjera" which clearly connotes FDI.

[12] The first question arguably has a positive frame in that it emphasizes FDI's potential to promote economic development. Hiscox (2006) shows, however, that positive framing effects do not bias responses to survey questions about international trade. Another possible concern with the first question is that it inquires about FDI's effects on the country overall rather than the respondent. This type of broad framing is common to virtually all survey questions used in research on international economic policy preferences. A previous version of this paper uses a Mexican survey question that inquires about FDI's effects for the respondent specifically and draws the same substantive conclusions.

[13] Unfortunately, more detailed data on respondents' labor market characteristics like industry of employment or rural versus urban location are not available. There are many observable implications to my theory that could be tested with these additional data. To my knowledge, there is no multi-country survey that includes both this detailed information and questions about FDI preferences.

[14] There is no information about postgraduate education but given that the top category accounts for less than 10 percent of respondents across the samples there appears to be little risk of underestimating the effects of higher education on preferences.

[15] Survey responses distinguished between partial and completed schooling. For each level of attainment individuals could also report incomplete school (for example, began higher education but did not complete). Those who report attaining an incomplete education

ordered categories but preserves the assumption that shifts between any
two categories have the same effect. Finally, I construct four separate indicator variables for whether the respondent's highest level of education is: a
university degree, a partial university education (ended without a degree),
post-secondary vocational training, or secondary school completed. The
omitted group is all educational attainment less than secondary school
completion. Hiscox and Hainmueller (2006) use a series of indicator variables like this to estimate the distinctive effects of a university education on
preferences. A comparison of these coefficients gives insight on nonmaterial sources of preferences. Recall that Hiscox and Hainmueller single out
a university education as a source of socialization and information about
economic flows. A positive and significant coefficient for only the univer-
sity-completed variable would support nonmaterial explanations whereas
a factor income explanation is more likely if the other schooling indicator
variables are also significant.

I examine the influence of job security on FDI preferences using responses
to the question:

Which is your degree of concern about being without a job or being unemployed
in the next 12 months?

Job Insecurity is a four-category variable for which higher values correspond to greater concern about job security. The expected sign is ex ante
unclear; there are instances in which FDI inflows raise the volatility of
labor demand but other instances, such as economic crises, in which it
counteracts other sources of volatility. The coefficient represents the net
effect on employment volatility on FDI preferences, controlling for FDI's
effects on wages.

Occupational information provides proxies for additional alternate
explanations. *Public Employee* is a binary variable equal to 1 for respondents employed in the public sector. Privatization and FDI are tightly
linked as governments often sell state-owned firms to foreign firms who
have the requisite capital and expertise to operate these firms as profitable
enterprises. I treat privatization as a special case of FDI resulting in a net
reduction of labor demand. Not only do foreign-owned firms introduce

---

are coded at the next lower level (for example, a respondent who reported incomplete
higher education is coded as having completed secondary school). This coding creates a
bias against a statistically significant correlation of education with the probability of FDI
support.

laborsaving technologies but they typically dispense with the many perks of public employment. Respondents employed in the public sector could be more likely to oppose FDI on these grounds.[16]

I estimate a series of probit models to consider the relationship between these variables and the probability of support for FDI inflows. All models include controls for respondents' basic demographic characteristics: *Female*, equal to 1 if the respondent is a woman; *Age*, the respondent's age; and *Married*, equal to 1 if the respondent is married or cohabitating. Models also include country-fixed effects to control for the myriad of country-level factors that can influence preferences. I first estimate a set of baseline models to test core hypotheses using all three years' data. I then exploit the richness of individual surveys to test the robustness of core propositions to different measures of key variables and additional sources of FDI preferences. Table 4.1 provides summary statistics for all variables.

The baseline model estimates, summarized in Table 4.2, demonstrate that skill level, as indicated by education level, consistently correlates with the probability of supporting FDI. This relationship is statistically significant and robust to the use of different measures of educational attainment as a proxy for the expected return to FDI inflows. Models with separate estimates for different levels of education show that the probability of supporting FDI inflows increases with more education, often quite dramatically. Respondents who have completed university are, depending on the sample, between 7 and 10 percent more likely to support FDI inflows than those who have not completed secondary school.[17] Those who have completed secondary school and have no further education are 3 to 4 percent more likely to support FDI than those who have not completed this level of schooling. The significant findings for educational attainment below a university degree support an income-based explanation over an economic information or socialization explanation. I consider further comparisons of these two effects in the next section.

The results are mixed for the alternate channels of FDI's income effects. *Job Insecurity* is statistically significant for only the 1998 sample, for which it has a negative correlation to the probability of support for FDI. The substantive correlation of job insecurity with the probability of FDI support is

---

[16] This is the best approximation of which respondents are at risk of losing rent income following FDI. A more pointed measure, like whether the respondent is employed by a state-owned firm, was unfortunately not asked in the survey.

[17] All expected probabilities are statistically significant at no less than the 5 percent level. Calculated based on Table 2, Model 3, 6, 9, and 12 estimates. All expected probabilities reported are calculated with *Clarify* (Tomz, Wittenberg, and King. 2003).

Table 4.1 *Summary statistics*

1995

Variable	Obs	Mean	Std. dev.	Min	Max
FDI Beneficial?	7834	0.797	0.4	0	1
Years of Education	8041	9.246	4.758	0	16
Education Level	8545	1.354	0.914	0	3
University Completed	8041	0.098	0.2975	0	1
Vocational Training	8041	0.1	0.308	0	1
Incomplete University	8041	0.09	0.29	0	1
Secondary Completed	8545	0.233	0.42	0	1
Writing & Numbers	8214	0.07	0.26	0	1
Works in Office	8225	0.066	0.25	0	1
Retired	9060	0.084	0.278	0	1
Retired*University Completed	8037	0.007	0.083	0	1
Retired*Incomplete University	8037	0.0027	0.0	0	1
Retired*Secondary Completed	8541	0.0118	0.108	0	1
Retired*Vocational Training	8037	0.0059	0.077	0	1
Homeowner	9019	0.6886	0.46	0	1
National Pride	8827	2.474	0.738	0	3
Right Partisanship	6678	5.495	2.628	0	10
Job Insecurity	8882	0.811	1.19	0	3
Public Employee	9060	0.1	0.3	0	1
Female	9036	0.527	0.499	0	1
Age	9057	38.7	15.84	15	99
Married	9042	0.597	0.49	0	1

1998

Variable	Obs	Mean	Std. dev.	Min	Max
FDI Beneficial?	16244	0.774	0.417	0	1
FDI Encouraged?	16476	0.78	0.41	0	1
Years of Education	17239	10.27	4.3	0	16
Education Level	17239	1.237	0.88	0	3
University Completed	17239	0.11	0.3	0	1
Vocational Training	17239	0.098	0.298	0	1
Incomplete University	17239	0.107	0.309	0	1
Secondary Completed	17239	0.191	0.393	0	1
Writing & Numbers	16732	0.029	0.168	0	1
Works in Office	16463	0.056	0.23	0	1
Retired	17319	0.07	0.255	0	1
Retired*University Completed	16789	0.007	0.085	0	1
Retired*Incomplete University	16789	0.0027	0.052	0	1
Retired*Secondary Completed	16789	0.01	0.099	0	1
Retired*Vocational Training	16789	0.0061	0.078	0	1

1998

Variable	Obs	Mean	Std. dev.	Min	Max
Right Partisanship	14095	5.57	2.954	0	10
Job Insecurity	17609	2.087	1.0	0	3
Public Employee	17319	0.098	0.29777	0	1
Female	17839	0.5132	0.499	0	1
Age	17839	38.14	15.159	0	98
Married	17572	0.574	0.494	0	1

2001

Variable	Obs	Mean	Std. dev.	Min	Max
FDI Encouraged?	16748	0.754	0.43	0	1
Years of Education	18135	7.818	4.928	0	16
Education Level	18135	1.20	0.895	0	3
University Completed	18135	0.062	0.24	0	1
Vocational Training	18135	0.07	0.256	0	1
Incomplete University	18135	0.087	0.28	0	1
Secondary Completed	18135	0.222	0.415	0	1
Retired	18135	0.065	0.247	0	1
Retired*University Completed	18135	0.0054	0.073	0	1
Retired*Incomplete University	18135	0.002	0.049	0	1
Retired*Secondary Completed	18135	0.009	0.099	0	1
Retired*Vocational Training	18135	0.003	0.058	0	1
National Pride	17970	2.549	0.728	0	3
Right Partisanship	18135	4.6	3.465	0	10
Job Insecurity	17917	1.82	1.22	0	3
Public Employee	18135	0.086	0.28	0	1
Female	18135	0.509	0.499	0	1
Age	18135	38.545	16.0072	16	101
Married	18078	0.557	0.496	0	1

quite small compared to that of educational attainment. Similarly, public employment has the predicted negative effect but is statistically significant in only some specifications. The negative sign on the coefficient is consistent with the theoretical claim that public employees are vulnerable to a loss of rents when FDI occurs in conjunction with privatization. Gender, although a control variable, merits brief discussion given its consistently negative and statistically significant coefficient. Across the three sample years, women are between 4 and 6 percent less likely than men to support FDI inflows. There are no theoretical reasons to suggest why women are consistently

Table 4.2 *Baseline results*

	1995			1998						2000		
	P(FDI beneficial?)=Y			P(FDI beneficial?)=Y			P(FDI encouraged?)=Y			P(FDI encouraged?)=Y		
	(1)	(2)	(3)	(4)	(5)	(6)	(7)	(8)	(9)	(10)	(11)	(12)
Years of education	0.029**			0.032**			0.028**			0.014**		
	(0.003)			(0.005)			(0.005)			(0.003)		
Education level		0.149**			0.146**			0.120**			0.075**	
		(0.014)			(0.024)			(0.021)			(0.019)	
University completed			0.286**			0.375**			0.276**			0.201**
			(0.055)			(0.063)			(0.069)			(0.066)
Vocational training			0.242**			0.187**			0.153*			-0.031
			(0.075)			(0.045)			(0.068)			(0.053)
Incomplete university			0.197**			0.206**			0.260**			0.109
			(0.054)			(0.061)			(0.065)			(0.061)
Secondary completed			0.156**			0.116**			0.103**			0.090**
			(0.044)			(0.041)			(0.036)			(0.034)
Job insecurity	-0.007	-0.003	-0.003	-0.063**	-0.062**	-0.063**	-0.044**	-0.045**	-0.044**	-0.022	-0.022	-0.022
	(0.015)	(0.014)	(0.014)	(0.017)	(0.017)	(0.017)	(0.016)	(0.015)	(0.016)	(0.014)	(0.014)	(0.013)
Public employee	-0.013	-0.034	0.000	-0.045	-0.038	-0.049	-0.094	-0.088	-0.092	-0.097**	-0.114**	-0.108**
	(0.073)	(0.089)	(0.082)	(0.042)	(0.040)	(0.038)	(0.051)	(0.049)	(0.048)	(0.033)	(0.036)	(0.036)
Female	-0.193**	-0.173**	-0.186**	-0.161**	-0.162**	-0.162**	-0.163**	-0.164**	-0.163**	-0.121**	-0.122**	-0.122**
	(0.050)	(0.049)	(0.048)	(0.038)	(0.038)	(0.038)	(0.039)	(0.039)	(0.039)	(0.027)	(0.027)	(0.027)
Age	0.002	0.002	0.001	0.001	-0.000	-0.001	0.003**	0.002*	0.002*	0.001	0.001	0.001
	(0.001)	(0.001)	(0.001)	(0.001)	(0.001)	(0.001)	(0.001)	(0.001)	(0.001)	(0.001)	(0.001)	(0.001)
Married	0.132**	0.101*	0.138**	0.054	0.049	0.054	0.012	0.007	0.017	0.026	0.026	0.027
	(0.045)	(0.047)	(0.052)	(0.036)	(0.036)	(0.036)	(0.029)	(0.028)	(0.031)	(0.033)	(0.033)	(0.033)
Observations	6759	7199	6427	15011	15011	15011	15220	15220	15220	16526	16526	16526

*Significant at 5%; ** significant at 1%. Probit coefficients with robust standard errors clustered by country in parentheses. All models include country-fixed effects.

opposed to FDI inflows but the result echoes an analogous gender divide over trade policy.[18]

These baseline results demonstrate reasonably well that factor price effects influence support for FDI inflows. I undertake a series of robustness tests to further investigate the sources of FDI attitudes. The 1995 and 1998 surveys provide alternate ways of measuring skills. One question inquires: *In your job, do you spend a lot of time writing or working with numbers?* A second question asks: *Do you work in an office?* Both questions capture dimensions of skill that may not derive from formal education but are nonetheless skills that multinational firms demand. In particular, these measures can capture skills gained through work experience. The second question is a proxy for location-specific services jobs that MNCs may have a particular need to fill in the course of doing business. These measures also approximate the standard definition of nonproduction workers provided in this chapter. The low correlation between these variables and education confirms that they are conceptually distinct from formal education: for the 1998 sample there is a less than .01 correlation between a university education and each of the alternate measures, for the 1995 sample this correlation is approximately .06 for both variables. *Writing & Numbers* equals 1 for respondents who either write or use numbers regularly in their work. *Works in Office* equals 1 for respondents who work in an office. Both of these variables should have a positive relationship with support for FDI inflows. Table 4.3 reports model estimates using these alternate measures of skill. Both proxies of skill are positively correlated with support for FDI inflows at conventional levels of statistical significance in five of the six models.[19] These findings further demonstrate that returns to skills, broadly construed, explain support for FDI.

The question remains of how skilled workers have to be in order to support unrestricted FDI in anticipation of greater returns to their skills. In order for me to build on these findings in Chapter 5's discussion of democratization and FDI I must confirm that there is not opposition to FDI along any point on the skill continuum. This is a possibility if MNCs introduce laborsaving technologies that, on average, reduce demand for relatively low-skilled workers. I address this possibility by estimating the baseline model with separate parameters for each of the sixteen possible values in the *Years*

---

[18] See O'Rourke and Sinnott (2001); Mayda and Rodrik (2005). Burgoon and Hiscox (2008) offer the explanation that women have a protectionist bias because they are less likely to be informed about economic policies.

[19] The coefficient on *Works in Office* in Model 6 is estimated less precisely than in the other models; its p-value is .07.

Table 4.3 Alternate measures of returns on FDI

| | 1995 | | 1998 | | | |
| | P(FDI beneficial?)=Y | | P(FDI beneficial?)=Y | | P(FDI encouraged?)=Y | |
	(1)	(2)	(3)	(4)	(5)	(6)
Writing & Numbers	0.157*		0.173**		0.204**	
	(0.077)		(0.063)		(0.076)	
Works in Office		0.123*		0.145*		0.096
		(0.059)		(0.058)		(0.053)
Job Insecurity	−0.013	−0.009	−0.128**	−0.127**	−0.094**	−0.088*
	(0.034)	(0.035)	(0.033)	(0.032)	(0.035)	(0.035)
Public Employee	0.025	0.016	−0.006	−0.021	−0.061	−0.075
	(0.106)	(0.101)	(0.036)	(0.039)	(0.052)	(0.049)
Female	−0.202**	−0.200**	−0.159**	−0.159**	−0.167**	−0.176**
	(0.042)	(0.041)	(0.041)	(0.041)	(0.042)	(0.039)
Age	−0.001	−0.001	−0.002	−0.002	0.000	0.001
	(0.001)	(0.001)	(0.001)	(0.001)	(0.001)	(0.001)
Married	0.106*	0.111*	0.045	0.039	0.015	0.007
	(0.047)	(0.046)	(0.037)	(0.039)	(0.028)	(0.028)
Observations	6907	6911	14457	14222	14649	14409

*Significant at 5%; ** significant at 1%
Note: Probit coefficients. Robust standard errors clustered by country in parentheses. All models include country-fixed effects.

of Education variable described above. This is the finest grained metric of skill level available in the survey. This version of the baseline model makes it possible to identify any reversals in FDI support due to consequences that are confined to a subset of the labor force.

Table 4.4 provides the estimates of this version of the baseline model for each of the four question-year samples. Depending on the sample the threshold for a statistically significant probability of FDI support ranges between seven and ten years of formal education. These findings are roughly consistent with the average educational attainment of low-skilled FDI employment described in the previous section. The probability of support increases with additional years of formal schooling, providing further confirmation of the material interpretation of education.[20] For the most

---

[20] Again, as mentioned in note 14 to this chapter, this model compresses the number of years of educational attainment at the top levels. This may account for why in some samples the probability of support is not strictly increasing with years of schooling.

Table 4.4 *FDI preference, disaggregated education measure*

	1995	1998	2001	
	P(FDI beneficial?) = Y		P(FDI encouraged?) = Y	
	(1)	(2)	(3)	(4)
Two Years of Education	−0.0531	0.0101	−0.0981	−0.155
	(0.103)	(0.167)	(0.154)	(0.0992)
Three Years of Education	0.0337	0.0266	0.106	−0.0474
	(0.132)	(0.0980)	(0.108)	(0.0577)
Four Years of Education	−0.0760	0.0470	0.0135	0.0476
	(0.0909)	(0.0937)	(0.101)	(0.0731)
Five Years of Education	0.0727	−0.00985	0.0748	0.0544
	(0.101)	(0.0909)	(0.0933)	(0.0459)
Six Years of Education	0.243+	0.139	0.0765	−0.0234
	(0.136)	(0.0871)	(0.0791)	(0.0527)
Seven Years of Education	0.240+	0.0785	0.0388	0.110+
	(0.122)	(0.0746)	(0.0849)	(0.0627)
Eight Years of Education	0.226+	0.145	0.0724	0.0374
	(0.125)	(0.102)	(0.0817)	(0.0505)
Nine Years of Education	0.201*	0.157+	0.0562	0.0737
	(0.0921)	(0.0931)	(0.0886)	(0.0493)
Ten Years of Education	0.165	0.0762	0.194*	0.0776
	(0.149)	(0.0884)	(0.0893)	(0.0717)
Eleven Years of Education		0.253**	0.176*	0.127*
		(0.0974)	(0.0855)	(0.0511)
Twelve Years of Education	0.315**	0.259*	0.211**	0.163**
	(0.0979)	(0.103)	(0.0758)	(0.0386)
Thirteen Years of Education	0.338**	0.360**	0.289**	
	(0.0882)	(0.102)	(0.0680)	
Fourteen Years of Education	0.553**	0.348**	0.280*	
	(0.0598)	(0.0962)	(0.115)	
Fifteen Years of Education	0.351**	0.338**	0.358**	0.145**
	(0.0902)	(0.0886)	(0.0829)	(0.0562)
Sixteen Years of Education	0.443**	0.498**	0.367**	0.230**
	(0.0480)	(0.0914)	(0.0937)	(0.0550)
Job Insecurity	−0.0119	−0.0619**	−0.0427**	−0.0216
	(0.0155)	(0.0171)	(0.0158)	(0.0136)
Public Employee	−0.0234	−0.0566	−0.0977+	−0.110**
	(0.0784)	(0.0387)	(0.0506)	(0.0359)
Female	−0.195**	−0.161**	−0.163**	−0.121**
	(0.0475)	(0.0376)	(0.0389)	(0.0267)
Age	0.00194	0.000401	0.00262**	0.00129
	(0.00136)	(0.00110)	(0.000976)	(0.00132)
Married	0.130**	0.0518	0.0170	0.0265
	(0.0494)	(0.0362)	(0.0305)	(0.0325)

(*continued*)

Table 4.4 (*Continued*)

	1995	1998		2001
	P(FDI beneficial?) = Y		P(FDI encouraged?) = Y	
	(1)	(2)	(3)	(4)
Constant	0.594**	0.317**	0.318**	0.190*
	(0.131)	(0.1000)	(0.0875)	(0.0766)
Observations	6,759	15,011	15,220	16,526

** p<0.01, * p<0.05, + p<0.1
Note: Robust standard errors in parentheses; Missing cells reflect education levels that are collinear with other levels.

part, respondents below the threshold are indifferent to FDI as indicated by the point estimates below conventional levels of significance (though often close). This finding shows that no subset of labor is opposed to FDI inflows. In Chapter 5 I link democratization to foreign ownership liberalization through labor support for FDI, and this finding confirms that labor is relatively unified in its support.

A final set of robustness checks draw on the richness of the individual surveys to specify expanded models that include a wider range of potential influences on FDI preferences. Briefly, I examine three additional factors using data for those survey years that include appropriate proxies. First, Scheve and Slaughter (2001b) show that homeownership is a distinct channel through which international economic flows influence individual income. To the extent that FDI flows improve local economic conditions they raise the value of geographically fixed assets like real estate. Model 1 in Table 4.5 includes *Homeowner*, a binary variable equal to 1 if the respondent is a homeowner. [21] The estimated coefficient is positive and statistically significant, supporting the importance of asset ownership in shaping economic preferences.

Second, existing research points to the negative influence of national pride on support for international economic flows. This argument is closely related to the earlier discussion of the socializing effect of education; individuals with a strong professed attachment to their country are perhaps wary of foreign influences. The 1995 and 2001 surveys provide another way of assessing this class of effects. These surveys include the question:

[21] This test is necessarily less precise than Scheve and Slaughter (2001b) because homeownership cannot be interacted with a measure of FDI's economic effects for respondents' community.

Table 4.5 *Expanded models of FDI preferences*

	1995	1998	1998	2001
	P(FDI beneficial?) =Y	P(FDI beneficial?) =Y	P(FDI encouraged?) =Y	P(FDI encouraged?) =Y
	(1)	(2)	(3)	(4)
University Completed	0.432**	0.395**	0.285**	0.197**
	(0.040)	(0.059)	(0.063)	(0.065)
Vocational Training	0.296**	0.184**	0.144*	−0.037
	(0.093)	(0.045)	(0.072)	(0.053)
Incomplete University	0.228**	0.201**	0.269**	0.111
	(0.046)	(0.071)	(0.070)	(0.062)
Secondary Completed	0.139	0.104*	0.088*	0.091**
	(0.073)	(0.048)	(0.042)	(0.033)
Job Insecurity	0.026	−0.118**	−0.076	0.011
	(0.048)	(0.035)	(0.039)	(0.043)
Public Employee	−0.032	−0.029	−0.058	−0.115**
	(0.059)	(0.043)	(0.053)	(0.038)
Homeowner	0.058**			
	(0.021)			
National Pride	0.151**			0.042
	(0.033)			(0.031)
Right Partisanship	0.044**	0.002	0.002	0.010
	(0.009)	(0.008)	(0.009)	(0.006)
Age	−0.000	−0.000	0.002*	0.001
	(0.001)	(0.001)	(0.001)	(0.001)
Married	0.127**	0.053	0.022	0.025
	(0.046)	(0.039)	(0.034)	(0.032)
Observations	4796	12155	12317	16397

* Significant at 5%; ** significant at 1%

How proud are you to be [respondent's nationality]? Are you very proud, fairly proud, a little proud, or not proud at all?

From responses to this question I construct a four-category variable ranging from 0 to 3; higher values indicate a stronger sense of national pride. Models 1 and 4 in Table 4.5 include the variable *National Pride*. Surprisingly, the coefficients are positive, indicating that respondents who express a stronger identification with their country are more likely to support unrestricted FDI inflows. The models include controls for respondents' education so the positive correlation, albeit small and statistically significant in only one model, likely reflects a global attitude about FDI and its potential to spur economic growth.

Third, studies of public opinion regularly find that respondents' political party exerts influence on preferences by providing informational cues and the pressure to remain loyal to the party (Kaufman and Zuckerman 1998). Accordingly, partisan affiliation may independently influence preferences for FDI inflows. All four models in Table 4.5 include the variable *Right Partisanship*, a variable that indicates where on a 0 to 10 scale of partisanship respondents place themselves; higher values correspond to the political right. I do not have an ex ante expectation about the sign of the coefficients. Partisanship in Latin America is sufficiently complex that a simple equation of right parties with capital's preferences or left parties with labor is ill- advised (Stokes 1996b). Only in Model 1 does partisanship have a statistically significant correlation, and the coefficients on the education variables remain substantively larger and precisely estimated. This shows that even when partisanship is correlated with preferences it does not subsume income's influence on preferences.

4.3 Conclusion

This chapter provides the first microlevel evidence that labor in developing countries supports unrestricted FDI inflows. The analysis takes into account a broad set of economic and political considerations that shape FDI attitudes. The empirical findings validate the claim that labor supports FDI and that skilled workers are more likely to express support because of their higher expected wages. The evidence for alternate channels for FDI's effects on labor income – job insecurity and public employment – is, at best, weak. Further, respondents' stated nationalist beliefs correlate with a higher probability of FDI support. The core findings are robust to alternate measures of skill and expanded models that include additional possible correlates of FDI preferences. Collectively, these findings reaffirm the basic theoretical foundations supplied by the specific factors model with regard to FDI's consequences for labor. More broadly, they provide a sketch of FDI's political and economic effects as seen from the individual perspective.

Despite the consistent and compelling evidence that labor supports FDI inflows there remains a popular perception that MNCs exploit workers in developing countries, paying low wages and committing gross violations of basic labor rights. This perception exists despite considerable evidence that MNCs adhere to better labor practices than domestic firms because of their need to attract the highest quality local workers (Brown, Deardorff, and Stern 2003, Mosley 2010). How can this perception be reconciled with this chapter's findings? This issue is complex, reflecting a variety of normative and material issues. I can offer one part of the answer based on theories about the political rights of labor in democracies and evidence about the type of FDI countries receive when ownership restrictions are in place. As discussed in Chapter 3, the MNCs that invest despite regulations tend to be less productive or transfer less productive technologies. The authoritarian governments that restrict ownership also offer incentives to investment in the presence of restrictions, including very low labor costs secured through government-sanctioned labor repression. Active labor repression gave way to expanded labor rights in new democracies including the right to organize politically. In the following chapter I provide examples of how labor unions, protected by basic political freedoms, could bargain with MNCs more credibly than was previously possible. In other words, FDI inherently raises returns to labor; historical examples of labor opposition to FDI reflect the host country policies that divert those returns to local firms and MNCs. Chapter 5 examines why antilabor policies regarding FDI like these fell out of favor once countries democratized.

5

Democratization and Cross-National FDI
Liberalization

At this point in the book hypothesized political alignments over FDI regulation are clear: labor supports unrestricted FDI, but local firms prefer regulations that require MNCs to share technologies with them. Chapter 3 provides a thorough discussion of why these alignments emerge, and Chapter 4 confirms labor's support for FDI empirically. With this theoretical foundation firmly established I turn to the book's central puzzle: why have countries grown more open to FDI inflows over time?

This chapter examines why the extent of foreign-ownership restrictions varies across countries and what about countries has changed to produce greater FDI openness. Recall Figure 1.2 from Chapter 1. The figure illustrates stark cross-country variation in the average percent of industries that countries protect from unrestricted foreign ownership. Developing countries (e.g. countries outside of the OECD) were responsible for the majority of regulations during the sample period of 1970–2000. The figure also demonstrates a steady decline in average extent of regulations over time. At the peak of regulations in the mid-1970s the average country protected 35 percent of its industries from wholly foreign-owned companies. By 2000 this figure had dropped to 10 percent. Explaining this shift in formal FDI policies requires attention to the policy makers that set regulations.[1] Political institutions provide the link between economic policy preferences and formal policy outcomes. Institutions structure politicians' incentives to favor one group's preferred policies over those of other groups.

Autocratic politicians privilege the interests of the narrow elite whose support is necessary to maintain political power. Autocratic leaders in developing countries are unaccountable to the majority of their populations

---

[1] See the Appendix for a discussion of the precise sources of national FDI policies (e.g. legislation, bureaucratic rules).

because institutional mechanisms that foster accountability – universal suffrage and contested elections – are absent. In the East Asian and Latin American countries that limited foreign ownership most extensively, this elite included a nascent industrial class that profited from FDI regulation. As detailed in Chapter 3, foreign-ownership restrictions require MNCs to form partnerships with host country firms as a condition of entering the market. Through these partnerships local firms access MNCs' firm-specific technology and production know-how needed for industrialization. These gains to local capital require a sacrifice by local labor. MNCs are less likely to invest in the presence of FDI regulations that weaken their control over productive assets.

Democratization shifts policy makers' incentives in the direction of FDI policies that serve the interests of labor. Democratization among developing countries during the sample period contributed to FDI liberalization by conferring greater political influence to labor. Democracies obviously differ in their precise institutional form, but they share a common emphasis on broad-based representation and accountability. Through a variety of mechanisms policy makers in democracies are more likely to enact policies that further labor interests than policies that favor local firms to labor's detriment. Chapter 2 describes specific mechanisms including politicians' greater accountability to voters and political freedoms that allow labor to engage in political lobbying. Figure 5.1 illustrates the tight inverse correlation between democratization and the average extent of foreign-ownership regulations. The dramatic increase in democratization is indicative of the "third wave" of democracy that began in the late 1970s and proceeded through the end of the century (Huntington 1993). The dashed line, indicating the number of democracies worldwide, illustrates the trend. In 1970 there were thirty-one democracies in the world; by 2000 the figure had nearly doubled to fifty-seven democracies.

Democratization in developing countries gave labor more political influence. Developing countries are, by definition, capital-scarce and labor-abundant such that expanded political participation works to labor's benefit. Following democratization policy makers have greater incentives to heed labor preferences. Figure 1.2 plots by region the number of democracies and average foreign-ownership regulations. Not surprisingly, the most dramatic fluctuations in regulation and democratization were in Latin America and East Asia, the two regions in which countries aggressively pursued state-led industrialization strategies. Democratization was only one of many sources of change in developing countries during the sample period, but I show empirically that democratization has driven liberalization, rather than the

Figure 5.1 Democratization coincides with foreign ownership liberalization.
Note: This figure plots the annual global mean of *Entry Restriction* and number of democracies worldwide (*Democracy* = 1). Excludes all Soviet bloc countries for the duration of the sample.

disciplining effect of economic crises, external donor pressure to liberalize, and more diffuse mechanisms by which countries adopt the policy changes of peer countries.

Before proceeding to describe the empirical tests and findings, a few words on how to interpret and measure democracy's effects are in order. My theoretical argument presents a rich set of testable implications about specific forms of political liberalization and their relative importance in generating policy change. In this chapter I focus on testing the broadest implications, democratization's effect on the extent of regulations. Only once we have sufficiently established that democratization does robustly correlate with regulation can we begin to investigate the mechanisms underlying this broad political transformation. I consider a number of alternate explanations that could coincide with democratization to confirm that the finding is not spurious. Additionally, I verify the finding's robustness to different measures of ownership regulation, democracy, and statistical models. The challenge in testing finer-grained mechanisms about political change is the absence of consistent data across this large a sample of countries. By validating the basic relationship I open up a new research program on the micropolitical economy of policy liberalization to structure inquiry into more nuanced features of FDI policy making.

5.1 Democratization and Foreign Ownership
Liberalization: A Baseline Model

The outcome of interest *Entry Restriction* is the percent of industries in a country-year subject to foreign-ownership restrictions, the country-level measure of restrictions introduced and used to estimate a model of FDI volumes in Chapter 3. This measure captures the extent of foreign ownership regulations in a country-year. "Extent" refers to the proportion of a country's industries that are protected from unrestricted foreign ownership. The data cover the period 1970–2000, and there are ninety-seven countries in the sample. Due to missing data most models are based on a somewhat smaller country sample.[2]

The country sample is intentionally broad, covering both developed and developing countries. Pooling these countries is appropriate because FDI's distributive effects of raising labor demand and lowering returns to local capital occur regardless of the host country's level of development. Below I show that my conclusions about democratization and FDI liberalization hold when those countries that have been advanced industrialized democracies for the full sample period are dropped from the sample. Below I compare the estimates of the baseline model to the same model estimated with *Investment Screening*, the measure of informal ownership regulations presented in Chapter 3.

My preferred measure of democracy captures the essential mechanisms through which labor exerts political influence in developing countries. *Democracy* is a binary variable that equals 1 when both the chief executive and legislature are popularly selected through contested elections. Four conditions must hold: popular election of the chief executive or selection by a popularly elected body, popularly elected legislature, at least two parties participating in competitive elections, and consistency in electoral rules during turnover of elected offices (Cheibub, Gandhi, Vreeland 2009, 69). This measure precisely captures the accountability dimension of democratization that connects democratization to increased adoption of labor-friendly economic policies. Additionally, changes in this binary measure can be interpreted as a switch between autocracy and democracy rather than changes in increments of democracy on a continuous scale. Figure 5.2 plots the annual average value of *Entry Restriction* for autocracies (*Democracy* =0) and democracies (*Democracy* =1). It illustrates a persistent gap in average levels of regulation between democracies and autocracies that is

[2] See Appendix for a full list of countries.

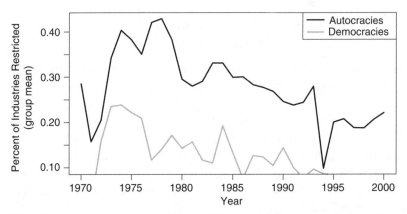

Figure 5.2   Average foreign ownership restrictions, autocracies versus democracies.
Note: This figure plots the average value of *Entry Restriction* for autocracies (*Democracy* = 0) and democracies (*Democracy* =1). See text for variable descriptions and Appendix for sources.

consistent with my argument. Below I show that my findings are unchanged if I measure democracy using the widely employed Polity measure in either its given form of a 20-point scale or dichotomized.

These data have a time-series cross-sectional structure in which the number of cross-sectional units exceeds the number of temporal intervals. In all likelihood these data violate multiple ordinary least squares (OLS) assumptions. Under these conditions estimates of a naïve OLS model would produce incorrect standard errors. Following Beck and Katz (1995) I estimate OLS models with panel-corrected standard errors to account for contemporaneous correlation and panel heteroskedasticity. I include country-fixed effects to control for omitted, time-invariant characteristics of countries and year-fixed effects to control for temporal shocks common to all countries in a particular year. With these fixed effects in the model I can interpret model estimates as the correlation of regime type with democracy over time within each country. The model also includes a panel-specific AR(1) correction to correct for serial correlation across error terms within countries. I lag all explanatory variables by one year to account for a delay between a change in a country's economic and political circumstances and a corresponding change in foreign-ownership regulation. Table 5.1 provides summary statistics for all of the variables used in this chapter. Definitions and data sources for these variables are provided in the appendix to this chapter.

Table 5.2 provides estimates of the baseline model of ownership regulations that includes two covariates: *Democracy* and the natural log of per

Table 5.1 *Summary statistics*

Variable	N	Mean	Std. dev.	Min	Max
Entry Restriction	2255	0.1955	0.3673	0	1
Investment Screening	1525	0.3427	0.464	0	1
Democracy	2976	0.442	0.4967	0	1
Currency Crisis	2911	0.3668	0.482	0	1
Banking Crisis	2911	0.17	0.3757	0	1
Sovereign Debt Rescheduled	2976	0.0631	0.2433	0	1
IMF Conditionality	2933	0.1397	0.3468	0	1
Average Restrictions – Language Group	2426	0.2	0.179	0	1
Average Restrictions – Colonial Origin	3131	0.262	0.240	0.0285	0.857
Polity-Binary	3131	0.4816	0.4997	0	1
Ln(per capita GDP)	2868	7.7656	1.59	4.442	10.86
Spain Colony	3131	0.1485	0.3556	0	1
France Colony	3131	0.099	0.2987	0	1
Belgium Colony	3131	0.0297	0.169	0	1
Netherlands Colony	3131	0.0297	0.169	0	1

capita GDP. The inclusion of GDP controls for a wide array of time-varying economic factors that correlate with countries' general level of economic development. The log transformation of the variable ensures that outlier values do not distort the estimate of average correlations. Model 1 shows a negative and statistically significant correlation between democratization and formal restrictions on foreign ownership. Substantively this finding shows that countries that were democracies in the previous year on average restricted 6 percent less of their economies relative to countries that were autocracies one year prior. The magnitude of this relationship is comparable to that found in analogous studies of trade liberalization following democratization (Milner and Kubota 2005, 126).

Scholars of trade policy raise the possibility that democratization does not generate true economic liberalization but rather a shift away from formal restrictions in favor of less transparent policy instruments (Kono 2006). Policy makers might seek to maintain policies benefiting local firms but try to conceal these policies from labor in order to avoid an electoral backlash. For example, policy makers could eliminate formal restrictions but mandate screening of all proposed investments and grant regulators

Table 5.2 *Democratization and FDI liberalization, formal and informal barriers*

	(1)	(2)
	Entry Restriction	*Investment Screening*
Democracy (t-1)	−0.0623*	0.0143
	(0.0304)	(0.0405)
Ln(per capita GDP(t-1))	−0.0912*	−0.267**
	(0.0443)	(0.0809)
Observations	2,112	1,470
Countries	97	72

** p<0.01, * p<0.05, + p<0.1
Note: OLS coefficients with panel-corrected standard errors in parentheses. All models include country and year-fixed effects and a panel-specific AR(1) correction for serial correlation. Constant terms not reported.

wide discretion to impose restrictions on a case-by-case basis. This may be particularly attractive to local firms because it makes FDI protection a private good that regulators can use to serve the interests of specific firms. Given that democratization likely raises the costs of collective action and lobbying, the move to regulation as private good is plausible. Figure 3.1, the plot of global averages of *Entry Restriction* and the measure of informal FDI barriers *Investment Screening*, already suggests that this does not occur. Although informal regulations are more common over most of the sample period, both types of regulations declined over time. The estimates from Model 2 confirm that countries do not replace formal regulations with less transparent equivalents following democratization. There is no correlation between regime type and the pervasiveness of informal regulations. This null finding confirms that the decline in formal regulations corresponds to a genuine reduction in ownership restrictions. This finding holds when all the models discussed below are re-estimated with *Investment Screening* in place of *Entry Restrictions*.[3]

5.2 Robustness to Alternate Explanations for FDI Liberalization

There are a variety of alternate explanations for why countries might liberalize FDI inflows. In order to convincingly establish that democratization

---

[3] See supplemental appendix for estimates of all model specifications in this chapter with *investment screening* as the dependent variable.

generates openness I specify expanded models that include controls for these possible alternatives. I address two categories of alternate explanations for liberalization: economic crises and external influences. These alternatives are among the most common explanations for countries' greater openness to the international economy. I verify that the correlation between democracy and ownership regulation is not spurious by estimating models that include these country characteristics.

Economic crises commonly precede the decision to liberalize economic policies. There are two mechanisms by which crises can contribute to FDI liberalization. Crises that occur in the absence of political change provide a window for authoritarian leaders to adjust without backlash. Alternatively, crises that precipitate democratic transitions have a similar dynamic but leaders enjoy something akin to a honeymoon period in which voters give them wider latitude to implement reforms (Cukierman and Tommasi 1998). Regime transitions spurred by crisis are more dramatic because crises empower opposition groups early in the process whereas noncrisis transitions are managed by outgoing elites who build in protection for their interests within more gradual democratic reforms. Specifically, crises disrupt alliances between leaders and business elites because leaders can no longer provide state subsidies to support business activities (Haggard and Kaufman 1995). In both scenarios crises overcome a generalized aversion to risky and uncertain policy changes (Fernandez and Rodrik 1991, Weyland 2002).

Following this logic, a leader may liberalize foreign ownership not because of greater accountability to labor but in response to sudden and severe economic downturns. In the throes of a crisis policy makers may liberalize in hopes of stabilizing there economies in the short-term by attracting export-oriented investments that will help to correct payments imbalances, or MNCs that will acquire ailing state-owned firms. Even autocratic policy makers may choose this path if a crisis poses a greater threat to their political future than incurring the wrath of local firms. Alternately, crises can also lower opposition to unrestricted FDI. Leaders often enjoy more latitude for costly economic reforms when reforms can address particularly dire economic circumstances. In the case of foreign-ownership liberalization, local firms affected by the crisis may have a greater need for foreign equity partners and be more willing to sell them majority shares of their companies (Aizenman 2005).

I control for the potential role of economic crises in ownership liberalization by including measures for three distinct types of crises: currency crises, banking crises, and sovereign debt crises. All three should contribute to lower opposition to liberalization, but the size of this effect can vary by the type of crisis.[4] I interact each crisis measure with *Democracy*. The interaction terms readily distinguish the average change, if any, due to crises in democracies and autocracies.

Table 5.3 provides estimates of models for three types of crises. Models 1–3 estimate the correlation between one type of crisis and liberalization for both nondemocracies and democracies. The coefficients on *Democracy* are the correlation between democracy and the extent of ownership regulation when there is no economic crisis. Across the three models *Democracy* retains its negative and statistically significant coefficient. These findings confirm that the observed correlation in the baseline models is not because autocracies are more likely to experience economic crises. The coefficient on the crisis variable in each model – currency, banking, or sovereign debt rescheduling – indicates the correlation between crisis and ownership regulations in nondemocracies, e.g. when *Democracy* equals 0. The three crisis variables have the expected negative sign; countries that experienced a crisis in the previous year have less extensive regulations than countries that did not have a crisis in the previous year. Only the coefficient for *Sovereign Debt Rescheduled* in Model 3 is statistically significant.[5] This finding shows that countries that were autocracies and rescheduled their sovereign debt in the previous year had, on average, approximately 2 percent less of their industries protected from foreign-ownership regulations relative to countries that a year earlier were democratic and rescheduled their sovereign debt. Aside from this finding there is no statistically significant correlation between regime type and economic crises. Model 4 includes all three types of crises and their associated interaction terms to confirm that democracies have less extensive regulations independent of whether they experience economic crises.

Economic crises may not transform the domestic politics of FDI regulation, but it can open the door to external pressures to liberalize foreign ownership. Specifically, crisis-ridden countries that seek external assistance

---

[4]   In light of scholarly debates on the role of capital-account liberalization in precipitating economic crises, I reemphasize that foreign-ownership liberalization is distinct from general capital-account liberalization. There is no evidence that FDI inflows contribute to the probability of economic crises.

[5]   In the absence of established measures of default itself, incidence of rescheduling through the Paris Club, a standing but informal body of creditor countries, provides an indirect proxy for sovereign defaults. This choice of variable does not introduce selection bias because, for much of its active history, the Paris Club has had a mandate to provide assistance to even the most heavily indebted countries in need of debt rescheduling. Additionally, the group meets monthly so there is not a significant lag time between default and rescheduling.

Table 5.3 *Average effect of democracy on ownership liberalization during economic crises*

	(1)	(2)	(3)	(4)
	Entry Restriction			
Democracy (t-1)	−0.0654*	−0.0947**	−0.0655*	−0.0733*
	(0.0324)	(0.0325)	(0.0305)	(0.0346)
Currency Crisis (t-1)	−0.0110			−0.0114
	(0.0152)			(0.0151)
Currency Crisis (t-1)*Democracy (t-1)	0.00787			0.00698
	(0.0201)			(0.0201)
Banking Crisis (t-1)		−.0283		−0.0172
		(.02111)		(0.0212)
Banking Crisis (t-1)*Democracy (t-1)		0.0221		0.0200
		(0.0313)		(0.0311)
Sovereign Debt Rescheduled (t-1)			−0.0243+	−0.0270+
			(0.0137)	(0.0148)
Sovereign Debt Rescheduled (t-1)*Democracy (t-1)			0.0460	0.0492
			(0.0300)	(0.0318)
Ln(per capita GDP(t-1))	−0.0828+	−0.194**	−0.100*	−0.0904+
	(0.0474)	(0.0486)	(0.0429)	(0.0469)
Observations	2,032	2,032	2,086	2,032
Countries	91	91	93	91

** p<0.01, * p<0.05, + p<0.1

Note: OLS coefficients with panel-corrected standard errors in parentheses. All models include country and year-fixed effects and a panel-specific AR(1) correction for serial correlation. Constant terms not reported.

for crisis stabilization often receive assistance contingent on domestic policy changes. The most common scenario for these contingencies is when countries receive loans from the International Monetary Fund (IMF). Beginning in the early 1980s the IMF frequently made loans to countries that required the recipient country to implement economic policy reforms aimed to reduce government spending and remove market barriers. A country that borrows from the IMF may liberalize foreign ownership as a direct IMF mandate or in order to comply with other mandates like privatization. Many developing countries lack sufficiently large domestic capital owners who can both raise the capital to acquire a state-owned enterprise and provide the technological upgrades necessary for profitable private production.

The presence of an IMF agreement can require foreign-ownership liberalization independent of political regime type. Alternately, democracies could be systematically more likely to comply with IMF requirements, and this is the mechanism through which democracies have less extensive regulations rather than the hypothesized change in policy makers' incentives. I empirically test for these scenarios by adding to the model *IMF Conditionality*, a binary measure equal to 1 if in the previous year the country signed an IMF agreement. Additionally, I interact *Democracy* and *IMF Conditionality* to estimate the average extent of ownership regulations in democracies under an IMF agreement. A statistically significant coefficient for the interaction term but not for *Democracy* itself would mean that the effect of democracy operated through a different mechanism than what I have hypothesized.

Models 1 and 2 in Table 5.4 incorporate the IMF measure into the baseline model. Countries that signed an IMF conditionality agreement in the previous year restricted ownership into approximately 2 percent less of their industries compared to countries not under such an agreement. Model 2 establishes that the effect of IMF conditionality does not differ between autocracies and democracies. The central finding regarding regime type and regulation is unchanged.

Beyond the dictates of multilateral donors there are other external influences on economic policies that could prompt countries to open more of their economy to unrestricted foreign ownership. Diffusion scholars point to mechanisms through which policy makers respond to the choices of their foreign counterparts (Simmons and Elkins 2004, Elkins, Guzman, and Simmons 2006). Policy makers can learn about the effects of policy reform or mimic the policy changes of countries based on a socialized view of appropriate or desirable economic policies. The testable implication of these mechanisms is that countries dismantle barriers to foreign ownership when they observe peer countries doing so. A correlation between the policies of peer countries is taken as evidence of diffusion processes.

There are several country characteristics that can form the basis for these implicit peer groups. I focus on two such traits that diffusion scholars have found influence countries' propensity to sign bilateral investment treaties: colonial origin and language group. Countries that share a former colonial power are more likely to look to each other to learn about the possible effects of policy reforms or as a model to emulate. These countries often share a common language, similar political institutions, and the continued

Table 5.4 *External sources of foreign-ownership liberalization: coercion, learning, and imitation*

	(1)	(2)	(3)	(4)	(5)
	Entry Restriction				
Democracy (t-1)	−0.0635*	−0.0637*	−0.0692*	−0.0623**	−0.0710*
	(0.0307)	(0.0313)	(0.0319)	(0.0215)	(0.0323)
IMF Conditionality (t-1)	−0.0183*	−0.0182+			−0.0116
	(0.00895)	(0.0102)			(0.0112)
IMF Conditionality (t-1)*Democracy (t-1)		−0.000500			
		(0.0220)			
Average Restrictions – Language Group (t-1)			0.144*		0.155*
			(0.0733)		(0.0749)
Average Restrictions – Colonial Origin (t-1)			0.139**		0.147**
			(0.0505)		(0.0521)
Spain Colony				−0.563**	
				(0.112)	
France Colony				−0.458*	
				(0.216)	
Belgium Colony				0.0755	
				(0.0647)	
Netherlands Colony				−0.445**	
				(0.134)	
Currency Crisis (t-1)					0.00169
					(0.0123)
Banking Crisis (t-1)					−0.0153
					(0.0189)
Sovereign Debt Rescheduled (t-1)					−0.00123
					(0.0139)
Ln(per capita GDP(t-1))	−0.0624	−0.0586	−0.119*	−0.0912	−0.107+
	(0.0467)	(0.0472)	(0.0512)	(0.0629)	(0.0555)
Observations	2,091	2,091	1,673	2,112	1,593
Countries	96	96	77	97	73
Year-Fixed Effects	Y	Y	N	Y	N

** $p<0.01$, * $p<0.05$, + $p<0.1$

Note: OLS coefficients with panel-corrected standard errors in parentheses. All models include country-fixed effects and a panel-specific AR(1) correction for serial correlation. Year-fixed effects are included as indicated. Constant terms not reported.

disproportionate exposure to ideas emanating from the former colonial power. Additionally, these countries are likely to compete for FDI to the extent that the countries present a similar profile of transactions costs and market tastes for potential investors. Many of these dynamics are present among countries that share an official language. Although there is overlap between countries' colonial and language groups, the language measure captures less direct cultural ties that are the basis for countries' affinity for each other.

Following the existing literature on diffusion I test for a positive correlation between the extent of regulations in a country and the average level of restrictions for all countries in its peer group, whether it be colonial origin (*Average Restrictions – Colonial Origin*) or language group (*Average Restrictions – Language Group*). The use of these two measures requires a slight modification to the parameters of the empirical model, the omission of year-fixed effects. Both of these diffusion measures are heavily trended so I opt to remove year-fixed effects.[6] Model estimates, reported in Table 5.4, show that both variables have a positive and statistically significant coefficient indicating a positive correlation between a country's ownership regulations and those of its peers. Democracy's negative correlation with ownership regulations is robust to the inclusion of these controls. Model 4 provides an alternate measure of colonial origin in the form of dummy variables for former colonies of Spain, France, Belgium, and the Netherlands. Former U.K. colonies and independent countries comprise the omitted group. This model treats the influence of colonial origin as fixed across time but allows the salience of colonial origin to vary by colonizer and permits the inclusion of year-fixed effects. The coefficients on colonial origin are negative and statistically significant for former colonies of Spain, France, and the Netherlands. Relative to the reference group, these countries have less extensive ownership barriers. Model 5 incorporates the full set of alternate explanations thus far. Due to the inclusion of the diffusion measures year-fixed effects are omitted. Democracy remains a significant correlate of ownership regulation in all five models.

5.3 Alternate Measures and Model Specifications

Given disagreements about the optimal way to measure democracy I establish that the main finding is robust to alternate measures of democracy.

---

[6] The correlation between time and colonial origin and language group are –.689 and –.391 respectively.

Table 5.5 summarizes re-estimates of seven of the previously described models with a binary measure of democracy constructed from the Polity IV database. In order to maintain consistency with the preferred binary measure I collapse the twenty-point Polity scale into a binary variable equal to 1 for countries with a Polity Score in the top range of 6–10 and equal to 0 for all countries below that threshold.[7] In each of the seven models *Polity Binary* maintains a negative and statistically significant coefficient. The substantive magnitude of this correlation is only slightly smaller than estimates generated with the preferred democracy measure. The coefficients on most control variables remain consistent; only the coefficients for the colonial origin dummy variables in Model 6 exhibit meaningful change. Table 5.6 provides estimates with the full twenty-point Polity scale, providing additional support for my claim.[8]

I also address the possibility that democracy is endogenous to foreign-ownership liberalization. As noted above, several studies have ruled out the endogeneity of democracy to trade and capital-account liberalization. It seems reasonable that foreign-ownership liberalization would follow a similar pattern. I address possible omitted variable bias and endogeneity of democratization to ownership policies by estimating an instrumental variable regression. My instrument for democracy is *Years Since Independence*, the number of years that a country has been independent. This instrument satisfies the exclusion restriction by the following logic: the longer that a country has been independent, the more likely it is to be a democracy. The length of independence, however, has no systematic bearing on how many industries into which a country chooses to limit majority foreign ownership. This variable has been used in analogous studies on democratization's role in trade and financial liberalization (Eichengreen and Leblang 2008, Milner and Mukherjee 2009). Table 5.7 presents the first and second stage estimates of this analysis. For both the baseline model and the full specification the coefficient on *Democracy* remains negative and statistically significant.[9]

5.4 Robustness Tests

I perform additional robustness tests that, in the interest of space, I summarize here (full results are available in a supplemental appendix). First,

---

[7] Findings are robust to setting the cutoff at Polity = 5 and Polity = 7.

[8] Results in supplemental appendix.

[9] The first-stage F-statistic for both models, equal to 21.46 and 39.70 for the first and second models respectively, meet the Stock and Yogo (2002) test for the rejection of weak instruments.

Table 5.5 *Alternate measure of democracy*, Polity Score–binary

	(1)	(2)	(3)	(4)	(5)	(6)	(7)
				Entry Restriction			
Polity-Binary (t-1)	−0.0546*	−0.0654*	−0.0506+	−0.05237*	−0.0552*	−0.0546**	−0.0543*
	(0.0259)	(0.0281)	(0.0258)	(0.0262)	(0.0274)	(0.0183)	(0.0271)
Currency Crisis (t-1)		−0.0127					0.00180
		(0.0160)					(0.0123)
Currency Crisis (t-1)*Polity-Binary(t-1)		0.00991					
		(0.0207)					
Banking Crisis (t-1)		−0.0140					−0.0169
		(0.0225)					(0.0190)
Banking Crisis (t-1)*Polity-Binary (t-1)		0.0110					
		(0.0287)					
Sovereign Debt Rescheduled (t-1)		−0.0269+					−0.00197
		(0.0148)					(0.0139)
Sovereign Debt Rescheduled (t-1)* Polity-Binary(t-1)		0.0464					
		(0.0298)					
IMF Conditionality (t-1)			−0.0171+	−.00189+			−0.0105
			(0.00891)	(−0.0106)			(0.0112)
IMF Conditionality (t-1)*Polity-Binary (t-1)				0.0043			
				(0.0215)			

	(1)	(2)	(3)	(4)	(5)	(6)	(7)
Average Restrictions - Language Group (t-1)					0.147* (0.0733)		0.158* (0.0749)
Average Restrictions - Colonial Origin (t-1)					0.141** (0.0510)		0.149** (0.0527)
Spain Colony						0.314 (0.238)	
France Colony						0.447* (0.12?)	
Belgium Colony						0.0689 (0.0688)	
Netherlands Colony						0.370 (0.293)	
Ln(per capita GDP(t-1))	−0.0851+ (0.0447)	−0.0844+ (0.0476)	−0.0538 (0.0474)	−0.0524 (0.0262)	−0.120* (0.0510)	−0.0831 (0.0642)	−0.107+ (0.0553)
Observations	2,117	2,037	2,091	2,091	1,673	2,117	1,593
Countries	98	92	96	96	77	98	73
Year-Fixed Effects	Y	Y	Y	Y	N	Y	N

** $p<0.01$, * $p<0.05$, + $p<0.1$

Note: OLS coefficients with panel-corrected standard errors in parentheses. All models include country-fixed effects and a panel-specific AR(1) correction for serial correlation. Year-fixed effects are included as indicated. Constant terms not reported.

Table 5.6 *Average effect of democracy on ownership liberalization (Polity Score measure)*

	(1)
	Entry restrictions
Polity Score (t-1)	−0.00704**
	(0.00254)
Currency Crisis (t-1)	0.00195
	(0.0125)
Banking Crisis (t-1)	−0.0161
	(0.0193)
Sovereign Debt Rescheduled (t-1)	−0.00205
	(0.0136)
IMF Conditionality (t-1)	−0.0108
	(0.0109)
Average Restrictions (Entry Restrictions) – Language Group (t-1)	0.142+
	(0.0752)
Average Restrictions (Entry Restrictions) – Colonial Origin (t-1)	0.144**
	(0.0537)
Ln(per capita GDP(t-1))	−0.114*
	(0.0564)
Observations	1,535
Countries	169

** $p<0.01$, * $p<0.05$, + $p<0.1$

Note: OLS coefficients with panel-corrected standard errors in parentheses. All models include country-fixed effects and a panel-specific AR(1) correction for serial correlation. Year-fixed effects are included as indicated. Constant terms not reported.

as noted above, I replicate all of the above models for the informal measure of ownership restrictions and find no systematic relationship between democracy and the extent of informal requirements. Second, I generate a binary version of the dependent variable that equals 1 if a country restricts more than half of all industries. This specification is more blunt, but it is less sensitive to possible measurement error in the number of industries a country has. I estimate a logit model with country-fixed effects; the substantive conclusion is unchanged. Finally, I estimate whether the results hold when I remove OECD countries to confirm that their generally high levels of democracy do not drive the observed correlation. The results of

Table 5.7 *Instrument for democracy: years since independence*

	Entry Restriction			
	2nd Stage	1st Stage	2nd Stage	1st Stage
Democracy (t-1)	−0.590**		−0.813**	
	(0.0866)		(0.272)	
Time Since Independence (t-1)		0.0115**		0.00765
		(0.00087)		(0.0016)
Currency Crisis (t-1)			−0.00258	0.00517
			(0.0172)	(0.01317)
Banking Crisis (t-1)			0.0322	0.050863
			(0.0289)	(0.018)
Sovereign Debt Rescheduled (t-1)			0.0325	0.0312
			(0.0343)	(0.0252)
IMF Conditionality (t-1)			−0.0682*	−0.0676**
			(0.0327)	(.01967)
Average Restrictions – Language Group (t-1)			−0.0516	−0.4916
			(0.155)	(0.0552)**
Average Restrictions – Colonial Origin (t-1)			0.0328	0.02007
			(0.0628)	(0.05143)
Ln(per capita GDP(t-1))	−0.0866**	−0.0386	−0.0492	−0.07403
	(0.0315)	(0.0288)	(0.0406)	(0.0327)
F-Statistic		21.46**		39.70**
Observations	2,043		1,575	
Countries	92		72	

** $p<0.01$, * $p<0.05$, + $p<0.1$
Note: Two-stage least squares estimates with standard errors in parentheses. All models include country-fixed effects.

the fully specified models hold when these countries are removed from the sample.[10]

5.5 Conclusion

The profound shift toward greater openness to FDI owes to an equally profound political shift: democratization across developing countries during the sample period 1970–2000. Democratization transformed

[10] See Figure 1.2 for a description of which OECD countries are in the sample.

policy makers' incentives to regulate foreign ownership. In autocratic developing countries, the most frequent users of regulations, policy makers restricted foreign ownership to provide the local industrial class with access to MNCs' highly productive firm-specific assets and a share of the income that they generate. Democratization incentivized policy makers to be more attentive to labor interests. Expanded franchise and opportunities for political participation elevated labor's political profile because they make politicians accountable to voters. Countries dismantled foreign-ownership regulations following democratization in line with labor's preference for unrestricted FDI inflows. My empirical analysis of this claim uses original foreign-ownership restrictions data for nearly one hundred countries over the period 1970–2000, one of the most comprehensive data sources of its kind.

The findings confirm that democratized countries restrict fewer industries than they did as autocracies. Countries did not merely shift from formal to less transparent policies that target protection to specific firms. Further the finding is not an artifact of other common explanations for economic openness including economic crises, the dictates of multilateral donors, or the choices of peer countries. Additionally, empirical tests verify that the results are not sensitive to model specification, or the measurement of democracy, nor does foreign-ownership liberalization contribute to democratization.

This chapter's findings help to explain the broad shift toward FDI openness that I described in Chapter 1. Figure 1.2 illustrated the stark difference in average ownership regulations between industrialized and developing countries. Most foreign-ownership restrictions have been in developing countries. In this chapter I show that during the period 1970–2000 these developing countries tended to be autocratic. These governments produced restrictive foreign-ownership policies for the benefit of the local industrial elite. In Chapter 2 I derived labor's preference for unrestricted FDI inflows and in the following chapter rigorously tested that claim. Democratization shifted leaders' incentives, prompting them to weigh more strongly labor's policy preferences. Democratization is one of the main reasons for overall greater openness to FDI worldwide. Chapter 6 turns to the second main source of FDI liberalization: the rise of FDI in the context of multi-country production networks that lowered the costs to FDI inflows to host country firms.

Chapter 5 Appendix

Any variable without a source indicated is generated from original data collected by the author and described in the text. The unit of observation for all variables is country-year unless otherwise noted.

Entry restrictions: percent of industries into which foreign owned firms are restricted to a minority share or are completely banned in a country-year.

Investment screening: percent of industries into which proposed investments by foreign-owned firms a subject to approval by the host government in a country-year.

Democracy: binary variable equal to 1 if chief executive and legislature selected through de jure and de facto contested elections. Source: Cheibub, Gandhi, Vreeland 2009.

Polity-binary: binary variable equal to 1 if Polity Score ranking from Polity IV database is 6 or higher. Source: Jaggers and Marshall 2004

Currency crisis: binary variable equal to 1 if nominal exchange rate depreciates by at least 25 percent and exceeds the previous year's depreciation by at least 10 percent. Source: Leblang and Satyanath (2008).

Banking crisis: binary variable equal to 1 if seven criteria for the size and scope of a banking crisis are met. Source: Caprio, Klingebiel, Laeven, Noguera (2005).

Sovereign debt rescheduled: binary variable equal to 1 if a country requests a rescheduling of medium or long-term public debt. Source: Paris Club (www.clubdeparis.org/en/).

IMF conditionality: binary variable equal to 1 for years in which a country has signed a conditionality agreement with the IMF. Source: Vreeland (2003).

Average restrictions – language group: average value of *entry restrictions* for all countries with a shared official language (minus the country in question). Calculated with official language data from Cao and Prakash (2010).

Spain (France, Belgium, Netherlands) colony: binary variable equal to 1 for countries that are former colonies of each respective country. Source: Cao and Prakash (2010).

Average restrictions – coloniwl origin: average value of *entry restrictions* for all countries with a shared colonial origin (minus the country in question). Calculated with colonial origin data from Cao and Prakash (2010).

Per capita GDP: annual per capita GDP. Source: World Development Indicators, World Bank.

Years since independence: Number of years that country has had full sovereignty. Source: Eichengreen and Leblang (2008).

6

The Organization of Multinational Production and Cross-Industry Variation in FDI Regulation

Countries not only differ in their propensity to regulate FDI inflows, but in general, independent of specific country characteristics, there is variation across industries in the frequency foreign ownership limits. In Chapter 1 I described the higher frequency of ownership regulation in service industries as compared to manufacturing industries. Over time the number of restricting countries declined in most industries but in 2000, amid unprecedented volumes of global FDI, ownership restrictions persisted, and the disparity between services and manufacturing remained. In order for my account of FDI liberalization to be complete and convincing I must explain why the FDI policy-making process generates variation across industries and what about this process has changed to lower overall levels but preserve industry variation. In this chapter I test the implications of my model of FDI's distributive effects for industry-level patterns in foreign-ownership restrictions.

Cross-industry variation emerges because of variation in local firms' incentives to seek regulations. In Chapter 2 I identified two ways in which MNCs organize their production across countries. In market-oriented FDI firms established largely self-contained production facilities in host countries in order to produce and sell goods within that country. This form of FDI allows firms to circumvent trade barriers and/or compete in foreign product markets for nontradables like most service industries. Export-oriented FDI reflects a global production network in which firms fragment the production process across countries to take advantage of lower production costs rather than replicating the process within each host country. Export-oriented FDI capitalizes on low trade barriers and transport costs.

Local firms in industries that receive more market-oriented FDI bear higher costs from unrestricted FDI inflows than industries in which export-oriented investments dominate. The former type of investments create competition among local firms for workers and customers whereas the latter type only raises competition for labor. All else equal, firms in industries that face multiple sources of competition have greater incentives to lobby for ownership regulation. The difference in local firms' incentives to lobby for regulation accounts for the higher frequency of regulation in service industries. FDI into service industries is akin to trade competition for these industries in which cross-border trade is not feasible.[1]

Ownership liberalization emerged over time because MNCs increasingly pursued export-oriented investments. During the sample period export-oriented FDI grew as a percentage of all FDI. Figure 6.1 illustrates this trend among U.S.-based manufacturing MNCs with data on where their foreign affiliates sell the goods that they produce abroad. A direct measure of an MNC's relative export-orientation is the percentage of its foreign affiliates' sales that occur outside of the affiliates' host country. The figure shows that the export-orientation of U.S. manufacturing MNCs in the aggregate increased approximately 10 percentage points during the period 1983–2000. In particular industries there was a complete reversal from predominately market-oriented investments to mostly export-oriented FDI. In Chapter 2 I gave the example of U.S.-based computer MNCs in which the export-orientation of FDI grew by more than 40 percentage points between 1977 and 2000. Table 6.1 reproduces Table 1.1, snapshots of the number of countries that restrict investment in each of twenty-one industries in 1978 and 2000, and adds to it the percent of all affiliate sales that occurred within the host country in the preceding year. These data make clear that the growth of export-oriented investment was primarily within manufacturing industries. Between 1977 and 1999 the average growth for manufacturing industries was 11 percent whereas the average growth for services was only 1 percent. Figure 6.2 juxtaposes the distribution of market-orientation across this sample of industries. It demonstrates the importance of disaggregating FDI by industry in order to reveal salient patterns. Although the median value of market orientation, indicated by the dashed vertical lines, did not change appreciably, the lower panel illustrates the broader distribution of U.S. MNCs' market-oriented distribution in 1999. In that year MNCs in five industries exported a majority of affiliate output out of the host country whereas previously they had sold a majority of their output in the host country.

---

[1] Consistent with this formulation the WTO's General Agreement on Trade in Services defines FDI as a form of "trade" in services.

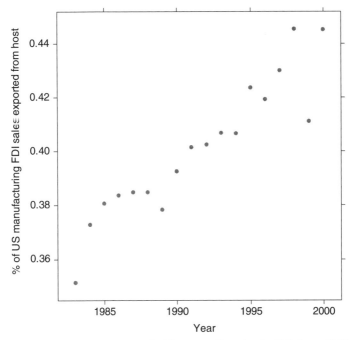

Figure 6.1 Growth in export-oriented FDI in manufacturing by U.S. firms, 1983–2000. *Note*: Figure plots data for manufacturing FDI by U.S.-based multinational firms. Points represent the percent of all sales by these firms that are made outside of the host country in which goods were produced. This is a standard metric of the export orientation of FDI. The plot demonstrates that export-oriented FDI as a percentage of total manufacturing FDI grew by approximately 10 percentage points between 1983 and 2000. Data are from *Annual Survey of Direct Investment Abroad* compiled by the Bureau of Economic Analysis, U.S. Department of Commerce. 1983 is the first year for which these data are available.

The rise of export-oriented investments weakened local firm's opposition to unrestricted foreign ownership. The growth in export-oriented investments contributed to the overall decline in restrictions and to the disparity between manufacturing and service industries in the frequency of ownership restrictions. To the extent that firms seek restrictions to shield themselves from product market competition, the shift to export-oriented investments reduces the need for such restrictions.

Further, industries in which local firms seek ownership limits to force technology transfer are less likely to receive FDI despite restrictions if FDI into their industries is more oriented to exports. MNCs typically can choose from a variety of markets in which to locate export-oriented investments

Table 6.1 *Growth of export-oriented FDI, 1977–1999*

	Market orientation of U.S. FDI	N countries with restrictions	Market orientation of U.S. FDI	N countries with restrictions	Growth of Industry export orientation
	1977	1978	1999	2000	1977–1999
Chemicals	0.739	13.000	0.638	6	0.101
Communications & audio and visual equipment	0.715	13.000	0.632	6	0.084
Computers	0.692	13.000	0.383	6	0.309
Fabricated metal products	0.769	13.000	0.737	6	0.033
Food	0.852	13.000	0.745	6	0.106
Glass and nonmetallic mineral products	0.724	14.000	0.774	6	−0.050
Instruments and related products	0.683	13.000	0.483	6	0.199
Motor vehicles, bodies and trailers, and parts	0.614	13.000	0.476	6	0.138
Nonmotor vehicle transport equipment	0.510	13.000	0.482	6	0.028
Paper products	0.627	14.000	0.756	6	−0.129
Printing & publishing industries	0.807	13.000	0.881	6	−0.074
Textiles, apparel, and leather products	0.651	13.000	0.571	6	0.080
Wood products	0.606	14.000	0.472	6	0.134
Manufacturing average					**0.117**
Finance except depository institutions & securities	0.889	22.000	0.713	15	0.176
Insurance carriers and related activities	0.882	20.000	0.825	23	0.057

	Market orientation of U.S. FDI	N countries with restrictions	Market orientation of U.S. FDI	N countries with restrictions	Growth of Industry export orientation
	1977	1978	1999	2000	1977–1999
Public utilities	0.980	19.000	0.990	14.5	-0.010
Real estate services	0.999	13.000	1.000	17	-0.007
Retail trade	0.980	19.000	0.985	13	-0.004
Telecommuni-cations	0.980	19.000	1.000	15	-0.020
Transportation	0.987	18.250	0.853	14	0.134
Wholesale trade	0.543	19.000	0.700	11	-0.156
Services average					**0.010**

Note: Data are from BEA (1977 Benchmark Survey) and BEA (1999 survey) and includes industries that were included in both surveys. In some cases industry categories had to be merged to make categories comparable: 1977 survey combined telecommunications and public utilities into a single category so the same value is entered for both industries. Computers 1977 value is for office machines; communications equipment 1977 is radio, television, and communications equipment. Noninteger values in public utilities and transport are due to averaging across multiple categories (public utilities = ISIC 40,41, transport = ISIC 60–63).

whereas the motives for market-oriented investment mean that countries with lucrative product markets can continue to attract investments despite regulations. MNCs with global production networks are more likely to utilize the firms' latest technology, which raises the potential costs of lost control over firm-specific assets. Recall from Chapter 3 that firms that invest despite ownership restrictions protect themselves by transferring out-of-date technologies.

I estimate a count model of the number of countries that restrict ownership into an industry in 2000. The outcome of interest, *Restriction Counts,* is the number of countries that impose foreign-ownership restrictions in a given industry. This measure collapses the country dimension in order to focus on industry characteristics that correlate with the frequency of regulation.[2] I interpret the correlation between general industry characteristics and the frequency of regulation as evidence of local industries' preference

---

[2] A country-industry model would provide richer insights, but the paucity of country-industry data make estimation of such a model unfeasible.

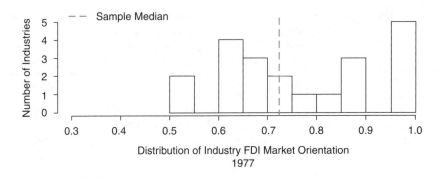

Distribution of Industry FDI Market Orientation
1977

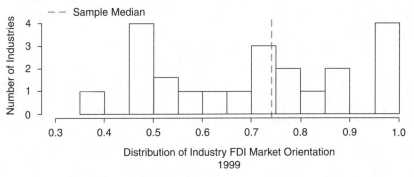

Distribution of Industry FDI Market Orientation
1999

Figure 6.2 Industry FDI market orientation, 1977 versus 1999.
Note: Histograms plot the distribution of market-oriented FDI for the industries listed in Table 6.2. Top panel plots data for 1977. Bottom panel plots data for 1999. Dashed line indicates median value. Data are from *Annual Survey of Direct Investment Abroad* compiled by the Bureau of Economic Analysis, U.S. Department of Commerce, and 1977 is the first year for which these data are available. See this chapter's appendix for additional details about industry categories.

for FDI while I control for other sources of correlation like the influence of industry characteristics on the cost of obtaining regulation.[3] Data limitations permit only a cross-sectional analysis, but the year of the cross-section, 2000, was among the lowest in average restrictions in the sample. An analysis of cross-industry variation when restrictions are at their lowest reveals why countries continue to restrict ownership in some industries in spite of the general liberalization trend.

---

[3]   One empirical finding in the previous chapter is that autocratic countries that reschedule their sovereign debt restrict ownership in fewer industries in the following year. A leader that liberalizes foreign ownership in response to an economic crisis may be more likely to deregulate export-oriented industries because exports help to correct payments imbalances. This motive may contribute to greater openness in export-oriented FDI industries but is unlikely to drive global patterns of ownership regulation.

The emphasis on industry characteristics allows me to further test the implications of the specific factors model of FDI's distributive effects. In this chapter my baseline model incorporates controls for industry scale, monopolistic competition in product markets, and the potential for productivity spillovers for MNC investors. These controls correspond to potential counterarguments for why local firms might be indifferent or even favorably inclined to unrestricted FDI into their industries. The findings in this chapter support my theoretical claim that local firms prefer restricted FDI inflows.

6.1 Modeling the Frequency of Industry-Level Ownership Restrictions

My empirical model of the global frequency of ownership restrictions by industry reflects several constraints posed by industry-level data. First and foremost, there are multiple industry classifications used in the collection of industry-level data. Empirical analysis, of course, requires that all industry-level data be measured in the same classification scheme. The differences between classification schemes are most prominent in disaggregated industry classifications; aggregate industry categories are typically more uniform across schemes. I reconcile the different classification schemes for the ownership restrictions data (ISIC Rev 3) and all other industry characteristics (NAICS 1997) by aggregating restrictions data to the broader classifications of the other industry variables.[4] I code the underlying country-industry observation as equal to 1 if one of the component subcategories is restricted.[5]

The outcome of interest, *Restriction Counts*, is the sum of these values across all countries in the sample. I use the raw data on investment screening requirements to construct *Informal Restrictions Counts*, a number of

---

[4]   Market-orientation data is organized by the U.S. BEA industry classifications, which, for 1999, were closely modeled on the 1997 North American Industrial Classification Scheme. I concord the restrictions data using an ISIC Rev 3-NAICS 1997 concordance from the BEA. See the appendix to this chapter for additional details on the industry classification of variables.

[5]   This is a coarser measure than would be ideal, but alternatives like calculating the percent of component industries is highly error-prone given the merging of data across different classification schemes. Further, each classification is not static but changes over time to reflect substantive changes in the nature of production. In light of these changes it is difficult to construct a meaningful time series.

countries that imposed screening requirements in each industry in 2000. I use this variable in my empirical analysis to differentiate between industry variation in the preference for regulation and industry variation in the cost of obtaining regulation.

The unit of observation in the cross-sectional model is industry, rather than industry-country, due to the absence of relevant country-industry level data for all but a few countries. Even if such data existed it is highly likely that country-industry characteristics are a direct consequence of foreign-ownership regulations, the outcome I seek to explain. Due to these constraints I estimate a count model that is comprised of only industry characteristics. I use U.S. industry-level data as a proxy for universal industry characteristics, a common approach to measuring cross-industry variation among a large set of countries (Rajan and Zingales 2003). The logic behind this choice is that the characteristics of U.S. industries provide a baseline for the relative differences between industries. Relative values across industries are likely to hold in a cross-national sample. Alternately, the U.S. data underestimates values for other countries, biasing the empirical analysis against my hypothesized claims. U.S. data, particularly for MNC activity, are more accurate than data from other sources.

The choice to estimate a cross-sectional model for the year 2000 is due to the availability of U.S. industry-level data necessary to measure the relative market-orientation of FDI in each industry. I use data from the U.S. Bureau of Economic Analysis' (BEA) survey of U.S.-based MNCs.[6] The 1976 International Investment and Trade in Services Survey Act requires these firms to complete a comprehensive survey about their worldwide operations every five years.[7] The BEA makes public country and industry aggregations of these data, and these are among the most comprehensive data available on the operations of multinational firms. The last year in the sample in which BEA administered the survey was 1999. The 1999 survey incorporated a new industry classification scheme that harmonized BEA industry classifications with widely used international classification schemes. These data are most consistent with the industry classification

---

[6]   The BEA is part of the U.S. Commerce Department.
[7]   The BEA interpolates data for the intervening years to generate annual estimates. These interpolated data are used in Figure 6.1. Pursuant to the act, the BEA must keep these firm-level data confidential, and they cannot be used as evidence against MNCs should they reveal breaches of U.S. law. This provision makes it more likely that firms will report accurate information. Firms face fines for not completing the survey.

scheme used to code the ownership restrictions data.[8] Independent of data constraints, the year 2000 is a substantively meaningful year for which to analyze industry-level variation. Figure 1.1 shows that in 2000 FDI flows were at their highest and average ownership regulations were at their lowest levels. The industries in which restrictions remained provide insight on which types of economic/industrial activities it remains relatively politically feasible to limit.

I use data from the 1999 BEA survey to construct a measure for the general market-orientation of FDI in each industry. *Market-Oriented FDI* is the proportion of total affiliate sales in an industry that firms make in host countries. This measure sums sales across all U.S.-based MNCs in the industry and all the countries in which they have affiliates, taking the sales patterns of U.S. firms to be representative of MNCs in a particular industry more generally.[9] The relative export-orientation of each industry is simply 1- *Market-Oriented FDI*. Sales-based measures of market-oriented FDI based on BEA data are standard in empirical FDI research.[10]

There may be concern that this measure of market orientation is, to some degree, endogenous to FDI restrictions. After all, ownership restrictions reduce the total amount of FDI that a country receives. It is, however, highly unlikely to be the case. For this to be true two conditions must hold: restrictions must deter one type of investment more than another, such that the overall distribution of sales between exports and local sales is altered; and this effect must be sufficiently robust to appear at the worldwide industry level, aggregating across all U.S. affiliates' production in that industry across all countries. The first condition is probable, but the second one is unlikely given that the choice of investment strategy is causally prior to the choice of host country.[11]

---

[8] Theoretically, it would be possible to generate a panel with five-year intervals, but since the industry classifications vary over time it would require aggregating both restrictions data and BEA sales data to high levels of aggregation.

[9] I assume that U.S. affiliates' sales patterns are representative of MNCs worldwide. MNCs' basic choice between export-oriented versus market-oriented FDI is generally the same regardless of the MNC's home country. This fact allows me to take data for U.S.-based MNCs as representative of MNCs worldwide. In more detailed aspects of production, there are some systematic differences across home countries. See Pauly and Reich (1997), Blonigen and Slaughter (2002).

[10] Brainard (1997), Carr, Markusen, and Maskus. (2001), Blonigen, Davies, and Head (2003), Hanson, Mataloni, and Slaughter. (2003), Yeaple (2003).

[11] For *Market-Oriented FDI* to be endogenous to restrictions it would have to be the case that the presence of ownerships restrictions prompts firms to switch from export-oriented FDI to market-oriented FDI, or vice versa. This is highly unlikely because such a switch

Industries into which market-oriented investments account for a larger share of total affiliate sales should have more countries that impose ownership restrictions. All else equal, local firms in industries that receive greater market-oriented FDI are more likely to lobby for regulations because they must compete with MNCs for both workers and customers. Local firms in industries that receive export-oriented FDI face lower costs from FDI into their industry. I test the observable implication of this claim that the industries in which a greater proportion of FDI was market-oriented in 1999 were regulated in more countries in 2000. Table 6.2 lists all of the industries in the dataset in descending order of how many countries imposed formal ownership restrictions in 2000. For each industry the table also shows the count of countries with informal regulations and the proportion of industry sales that were in the host country in 1999. These data underscore the persistence of foreign-ownership regulation in services industries.

The empirical model incorporates controls for a number of industry characteristics that could influence the net cost of FDI to local firms or their ability to organize and lobby for ownership regulations.[12] These controls are further tests of my model of FDI's distributive effects. As noted in Chapter 2, local firms may vary in their FDI preferences because industry characteristics can shield firms from MNC competition and perhaps even generate net gains for local firms via productivity spillovers. In order to interpret the correlation between market orientation of FDI and the frequency of regulation as evidence that local firms oppose unrestricted FDI, I must verify that these industry characteristics do not, in fact, make local firms in some industries *prefer* unrestricted FDI inflows.

Industries vary in the degree that firms compete for customers. In monopolistically competitive industries, firms' products are not perfect substitutes for one another. Firms carve out market segments by differentiating their products from those of other producers in the industry. The automobile industry is a classic example: although all firms produce autos, there is wide variation in their characteristics. In industries with greater product differentiation the entry of a foreign-owned firm may pose less of a threat to market share because the MNC competes in a different market segment. In many industries firms achieve product differentiation through advertising. Advertising is the vehicle used to inform consumers about the

would not evade the restriction nor would it meet the firms' initial goals. An MNC faced with an entry barrier will seek a market with a more liberal FDI regime rather than fundamentally change its investment strategy in order to invest in a country with restrictions. Additionally, because this measure aggregates data for all U.S. MNCs in an industry, it is less likely to be influenced by the policies of specific countries.

[12] The cross-sectional model precludes inclusion of industry-fixed effects.

Table 6.2 *Cross-industry distribution of FDI regulation, 2000*

BEA industry category	Restriction counts	Informal restriction counts	Market-oriented FDI (1999)
Transportation and warehousing	27	14	0.85
Telecommunications	25	14	1
Motion picture and sound recording industries & broadcasting	21	11	
Other finance, except depository institutions & securities	17	20	0.71
Insurance carriers and related activities	15	15	0.82
Professional services; management	11	23	0.826
Utilities	11	9	0.99
Printing & publishing industries	10	11	0.88
Construction	8	7	1
Machinery	8	13	0.60
Administration, support, and waste management	7	8	0.94
Other-transportation equipment	7	11	0.48
Retail trade	7	8	0.984
Hotels & restaurants	6	9	
Real estate	6	11	1
Wholesale trade	6	9	0.699
Beverages and tobacco products	5	12	0.667
Chemicals	5	11	0.6383
Communications & audio and visual equipment	5	11	
Computers	5	11	0.383
Fabricated metal products	5	11	0.736
Food	5	11	0.745
Furniture and related products; misc. manufacturing	5	11	0.642
Health care and social assistance	5	10	0.997
Information services and data processing services	5	7	0.896
Instruments	5	11	0.48
Miscellaneous services	5	8	1
Motor vehicles, bodies and trailers, and parts	5	9	0.476
Nonmetallic mineral products	5	11	0.774
Paper	5	11	0.756
Petroleum and coal products	5	11	0.835
Plastics and rubber products	5	11	0.67
Rental and leasing (except real estate)	5	7	1
Textiles, apparel, and leather products	5	11	0.570
Wood products	5	11	0.47

Note: See chapter appendix for notes on data sources and variable definitions. Blank cells in *Market-Oriented FDI (1999)* indicate industries for which necessary data were suppressed for privacy reasons.

distinctive features of a firm's product. It is a common measure of product differentiation (Bagwell 2007; Schmalensee 1989). Industries in which firms spend more on advertising as a percentage of sales may face less direct product market competition from MNCs and therefore be less interested in restricting FDI inflows. Firms in these industries may also vary in their preference for formal and informal regulation because they prefer more precisely targeted protection.

Industries also vary in their ability to capture productivity spillovers from MNCs. In Chapter 2 I noted the possibility that local firms can become more productive following MNC entry into their industry. Even when local firms are not in a joint venture with the MNC they can become more productive by observing the MNCs' production at close proximity or by hiring domestic workers who previously worked for the MNC. In industries with greater capacity to absorb spillovers there could be support for unrestricted FDI inflows. Industries in which firms have relatively high research and development expenditures to sales ratios have greater capacity to absorb spillovers, because they have the internal capacity to adapt technology and practices for their own use (Sembenelli and Siotis 2008).

Both *US Advertising Costs/Sales* and *US R&D Costs/Sales* are the median value for U.S. firms in each industry between 1990–2000. Again, I take the value for U.S. firms to be representative of the industry worldwide. I calculate these measures using data from Standard and Poor's Compustat North America – Industry Annual Data database of all public firms in the United States. The use of public firms makes these estimates optimistic – private firms are likely to be smaller and face a bigger threat from MNC entry into their industry. See the appendix to this chapter for additional information about these variables.

Finally, I control for the ease with which industries can overcome barriers to collective action in order to lobby for ownership regulations. Industry variation in the frequency of foreign-ownership regulation can reflect not only varied preferences for restrictions but also systematic differences across industries in the costs of organizing firms to lobby for regulation. As is standard in studies of trade policy, I control for industry concentration in order to capture the ease with which an industry can organize for protection (Baldwin 1985, Trefler 1993). *U.S. 4-firm concentration ratio*, my measure of industry concentration, is the four-firm concentration ratio for U.S. industries in 1997, the percent of total market share held by the four largest firms in the industry. *U.S. 8-firm concentration ratio* is the eight-firm concentration ratio and provides a more inclusive measure of industry concentration. These data are from the U.S. Census Bureau's Economic Census that is conducted at five-year

Table 6.3 *Summary statistics*

Variable	N	Mean	Std dev	Min	Max
Restriction Counts	36	7.972222	5.906346	0	27
Informal Restriction Counts	36	10.88889	3.926305	0	23
Market-Orientated FDI	32	0.7670897	0.1891323	0.3830092	1
U.S. Advertising Costs /sales	32	0.0176761	0.0198621	0	0.0788231
U.S. R&D Costs/Sales	33	0.0328635	0.0669833	0	0.3426872
U.S. 4-Firm Concentration Ratio	32	21.22188	15.97134	2.9	57.2
U.S. 8-Firm Concentration Ratio	32	29.25625	19.59867	4.1	71.9

intervals; 1997 was the most recent survey prior to 2000. [13] The U.S. data is often used as a baseline for the "natural" concentration of industries because concentration data for other countries is likely to be greater and reflect distortions created by policies that influence the costs of entry and exit of firms. The concentration measure also accounts for the presence of natural monopolies and the distinctive motives that countries can have for limiting foreign ownership in these sectors. This is an important control variable because countries regularly justify ownership restrictions in natural monopoly industries, like infrastructure, for public-interest reasons.

I estimate a negative binomial model with robust standard errors of *Restrictions Count*, the number of countries with foreign-ownership restrictions in a given industry in 2000. Among count models the negative binomial best reflects the variance in the distribution of counts across industries. Table 6.3 provides summary statistics for all variables.

Table 6.4 provides estimates of the baseline model. In Model 1, as anticipated, the coefficient for *Market-Oriented FDI* is positive and statistically significant. Figure 6.3 plots predicted counts of restricting countries across the range of observed *Market-Oriented FDI* values. The superimposed histogram displays the distribution of *Market-Oriented FDI* values in the data. At the lowest level of market orientation is the computer industry at 38 percent of total affiliate sales within the host country. Holding all other parameters at their means, the model predicts that three countries restrict

---

[13] These raw data are classified by 1997 NAICS; they were converted to the BEA classification scheme with an original concordance.

Table 6.4 *Sources of cross-industry variation in foreign-ownership restrictions*

	(1)	(2)
	Restriction counts	
Market-Oriented FDI	1.519**	1.414**
	(0.465)	(0.386)
U.S. Advertising Expenditures/Sales	−6.887+	−7.217*
	(3.672)	(3.656)
U.S. Research and Development/Sales	2.705**	2.519*
	(0.981)	(1.094)
U.S. 4-Firm Concentration Ratio	0.0202**	
	(0.00776)	
U.S. 8-Firm Concentration Ratio		0.0152**
		(0.00543)
Constant	0.419	0.486
	(0.425)	(0.368)
Observations	27	27

** $p<0.01$, * $p<0.05$, + $p<0.1$
Note: Negative binomial estimates. Robust standard errors in parentheses.

foreign ownership into the industries with the least market-oriented FDI. For industries in which all FDI is market seeking, including telecommunications, construction, and real estate, the predicted count of restricting countries is nearly triple. This variation in predicted counts in line with higher levels of market orientation provides initial evidence in support of my claim that countries more often regulate ownership into industries that get market-seeking FDI because of the higher cost of FDI to local firms in these industries.

The model estimates for the control variables verify that this finding is not an artifact of other industry characteristics that may correlate with market orientation. More generally, it further validates the specific factors model of FDI's distributive effects presented in Chapter 2. Industries with higher levels of product differentiation are restricted in fewer countries. This finding, statistically significant with a p-value=.061, provides some evidence that the net effect of product differentiation is to lower the cost of FDI-induced product market competition. The result confirms that the frequency with which countries regulate FDI into an industry corresponds to the magnitude of its costs to local firms. Below I discuss further monopolistic competition and local firms' incentives to lobby for ownership regulation.

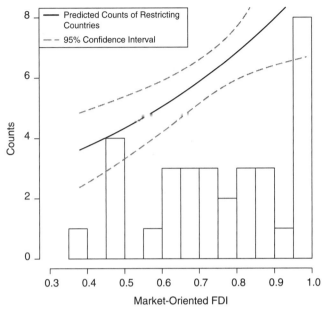

Figure 6.3 Predicted counts of restricting countries.

Note: The figure plots predicted counts based on Table 6.4 Model 1 estimates. Histogram provides distribution of *Market-Oriented FDI* for all industries in the dataset for which it is available (see Table 6.2 for a list). The y-axis measures industry counts with regard to the histogram and predicted country counts for the curve/confidence intervals.

More countries regulate ownership in industries with concentrated ownership. This finding holds for narrow (*U.S. 4-Firm Concentration Ratio*) and broad (*U.S. 8-Firm Concentration Ratio*) definitions of concentration in Models 1 and 2 respectively. Industry concentration accounts for plausible alternate explanations for industry level variation. Concentrated industries face lower costs to collective action because coordination and monitoring compliance are easier with fewer firms. Concentration is also an indicator of industries that are natural monopolies. As discussed in Chapter 1, politicians often justify ownership regulations on public interest and national security grounds. Even if these justifications are sincere and not a cover for rent seeking, these model estimates confirm that the market orientation of investments correlates with the frequency of regulation independent of their propensity to be natural monopolies.

Finally, the model reveals that countries more frequently regulate industries in which firms spend, on average, more toward research and development. This variable captures the unique preferences of firms that expect positive productivity spillovers; firms that may prefer unrestricted FDI inflows to maximize these spillovers. In Chapter 2, I flagged this as a potential counterargument to my claim that local firms oppose unrestricted FDI. I discussed that productivity spillovers obtain, at best, in the long term and following substantial adjustment costs to local firms. The implication of the counterargument is that fewer countries should restrict ownership in these industries because firms would oppose restrictions. The model yields the opposite result, that industries in which firms spend more on research and development are restricted in more countries, all else equal. This finding weakens the counterargument and, if anything, supports the basic purpose of ownership restrictions as a regulatory instrument. Industries with higher levels of firm research spending are precisely the industries in which access to MNCs' firm-specific assets is most lucrative.

6.2 Industry-Level Regulation – Robustness Tests

In Chapter 5 I discussed the possibility that countries replace formal ownership regulations with informal barriers that require all proposed investments to be approved by the government. I confirmed that democracies do not prefer informal barriers to obscure regulation from public view, an argument made by some trade scholars. Here I return to informal FDI barriers to examine whether some industries systematically prefer them to formal ownership regulations because they make FDI restrictions a private good.

From the perspective of individual firms, industry-level regulations like formal ownership regulations are public goods. All firms in the industry enjoy the protection of formal regulations regardless of whether they contributed to the political lobbying efforts necessary to secure the policies. Investment screening requirements make FDI regulation a private good because they allow policy makers to target regulations more precisely, blocking specific investments that threaten the interests of a single domestic firm. As I discuss in Chapter 2 trade policy scholars argue that countries often protect firms in monopolistically competitive industries from trade competition despite a market structure that should weaken the actual threat. The explanation for this trend is that the firm's lobbying costs are very low when seeking forms of trade protection that constitute private goods, like antidumping judgments.

I test the implications of this argument for FDI regulation by estimating a model of *Informal Restriction Counts*, counts of the number of countries that had informal screening requirements for a given industry in 2000. This

Table 6.5 *Sources of Cross-industry variation in informal FDI regulations*

	(1)	(2)
	Informal Restriction Counts	
Market-Oriented FDI	−0.101	−0.104
	(0.21)	(0.205)
U.S. Advertising Expenditures/Sales	−3.527	−3.584
	(2.459)	(2.442)
U.S. R&D/Sales	0.499	0.464
	(0.676)	(0.681)
U.S. 4-Firm Concentration Ratio	0.00198	
	(0.00401)	
U.S. 8-Firm Concentration Ratio		0.00181
		(0.00262)
Constant	2.490**	2.484**
	−0.159	−0.149
Observations	27	27

** p<0.01, * p<0.05, + p<0.1

Note: Negative binomial estimates. Robust standard errors in parentheses.

variable is identical to the main variable of interest *Restriction Counts* except for counts are of screening requirements rather than formal ownership limits. Evidence in support of this trend would be a positive and statistically significant coefficient for *Market-Oriented FDI*. Table 6.5 provides estimates of the same two versions of the count models but for counts of informal regulations. The estimates indicate that neither the extent of monopolistic competition in an industry nor the market orientation of FDI has a bearing on how many countries choose to screen proposed investments.[14] How to reconcile the finding that, on average, monopolistically competitive industries do not have more foreign ownership regulations with the existing contradictory finding on trade policy? The different preference alignments over trade and FDI policy provide one explanation. Labor support for unrestricted FDI is a counterweight to local firms' preference for

---

[14] In an alternate model specification (results not reported) I include the interaction of *Market-Oriented FDI* and *U.S. 4-firm concentration ratio*. The interaction provides a more precise test of the counterargument; firms in monopolistically competitive industries that experience local product market competition should have the greatest incentive to lobby for broad screening requirements that allow regulators to grant targeted protection. The sign on the interaction term is negative but below conventional levels of statistical significance (p-value=.14).

regulation, whereas specific labor and capital both prefer trade restrictions. In the latter case the private-good nature of regulation lowers the cost of securing the policies even if the distributive costs of trade openness are low. Even when FDI regulation can be a private good, as in the case of screening requirements, there is a constituency that opposes regulation.

6.3 Conclusion

The fragmentation of global production contributed to global FDI liberalization by lowering the distributive costs of FDI inflows to local firms in certain manufacturing industries. In the 1970s, at the beginning of the sample period, most MNCs organized multinational production to compete in foreign product markets. Local firms in industries that receive market-oriented FDI compete with MNCs for both workers and customers. These investments are the functional equivalent of trade flows; MNCs substitute FDI for trade when trade is costly or not possible.

Over the following decades the precipitous decline of transport costs and trade barriers made possible a second form of multinational production in which MNCs fragmented the production process across countries to take advantage of lower production costs. In export-oriented investments FDI and trade are complements – both are necessary for multi-country production networks to function. From the perspective of local firms these export-oriented investments were less of a threat because they do not introduce product market competition. Local firms in these industries have lower incentives to lobby for foreign ownership restrictions than their counterparts in industries that receive predominantly market-oriented FDI. The growth of export-oriented FDI weakened demand for ownership restrictions. This basic change in how firms produce goods and services in the global economy, in addition to democratization and its effects on policy makers' incentives, is responsible for countries' greater openness to FDI inflows.

This chapter's findings confirm my claim in Chapter 2 that local firms oppose FDI into their industries. This claim follows from the implications of the specific factors model: local firms' labor costs rise and, in some cases, product market competition increases. The empirical model in this chapter includes controls for multiple industry characteristics that fall outside of the specific factors model and that may moderate or even reverse FDI's hypothesized consequences for local firms. I show that ownership restrictions remain more common the more that FDI into the industry is market-oriented, even when account is taken of an industry's product differentiation, ability to capture productivity spillovers from MNCs, and barriers to collective action. Although these alternate explanations do not have as much bearing on the frequency of restrictions, the finding that regulations are less common in industries with product differentiation is consistent with the weaker threat of product market competition in monopolistically competitive industries

The persistence of ownership restrictions in service industries points to FDI's role in integrating service industries into the international economy. Despite some growth in cross-border services trade (e.g. call centers, lower skill business services), most service industries still require the provider to have a physical presence in the host economy. FDI into services introduces international competition into industries that are otherwise shielded from foreign competition. Service MNCs, like all MNCs, are more productive than their local counterparts and usually compete with local firms on price and quality. The data presented in this chapter shows that at the end of the twentieth century there remained substantial barriers to international competition in services. The lack of FDI openness in these industries significantly limits the depth of international economic integration.

Chapter 6 Appendix

Market Orientation of FDI

Data on the sales of U.S.-based multinational corporations are from the BEA 1999 Survey of Direct Investment Abroad. Any data suppressed for privacy reasons are designated as missing (indicated by "(D)" in the original BEA data). Data for which values are close to zero, noted as varying between –US$500,000 and US$500,000 (indicated by "(*)" in the original dataset) are set at their maximum value. In order to use these data, industry designations have to be aggregated up from the ISIC Rev 3 into the BEA's classifications scheme, a variation of the 1997 NAICS.[15] In some instances aggregation required summing across categories that include suppressed data, creating estimates that are lower than their true values.

Advertising and R&D Expenditures

Data are from Standard and Poor's Compustat North America Industry Annual Data database. The database includes all publicly traded U.S. firms listed on one of three major stock exchanges. Advertising expenditures as a percentage of total sales was calculated for all firms in the database that provided this information. The variable used is, for each industry, the median ratio of advertising (research and development) expenditures to sales from 1990–2000.

Industry Concentration

Four and eight-firm concentration ratios for U.S. industries in 1997 are from the U.S. Census Bureau. These raw data are classified by 1997 NAICS, they were converted to the BEA classification scheme with an original concordance.

---

[15] Data on ownership restrictions were originally classified by the International Standard Industrial Classification Revision 3 (ISIC Rev 3), standardized to the two-digit aggregation. I constructed a correspondence between ISIC Rev 3 and the BEA's industrial classification for international surveys to use the BEA's industry-level sales data. This correspondence is available upon request.

7

The Politics of FDI in the Twenty-First Century

FDI stands at the heart of current international economic integration. These investments by multinational firms exceed the monetary value of all other forms of international capital flows by a large margin. These firms generate the majority of world trade. Trade among subsidiaries of the same firm during the production process alone accounts for more than one-third of all international trade. FDI has unparalleled potential to promote industrialization through technology transfer and also contributes to stabilization in countries in the aftermath of economic crises. Multinational firms also feature prominently in controversies regarding economic globalization as evident in persistent questions about their evasion of national laws and, sometimes, even basic human-rights standards.

Despite FDI's central and varied role in the international economy there is little understanding of the underlying political and economic shifts responsible for its prominence. There were strident debates in the 1960s and 1970s over the role of MNCs in developing countries. Sharply ideological rhetoric equated FDI with imperialism that would render developing countries permanently underdeveloped. By the end of the twentieth century there had been a dramatic reversal in attitudes toward FDI. Countries that previously limited MNCs' participation in their economies went to enormous lengths to entice FDI, offering all manner of subsidies and more favorable regulatory standards than were available to domestic firms. Political economy scholarship on FDI has been overwhelmingly focused on questions of FDI supply – how politics influences firms' investment location decisions – rather than questions of countries' FDI demand as manifest in citizens' attitudes and formal FDI policies. These supply-side theories lack the ability to explain why countries' openness to FDI would change over time.

This book provides precisely such a demand-side theory that directly focuses on the politics of FDI from the perspective of recipient countries instead of that of MNCs. By taking account of the motives for and organization of investments my theory of FDI's distributive effects pinpoints sources of variation in support for FDI across countries and industries. Labor and capital divide over FDI, because FDI inflows raise wages but create competition for local producers. Two larger political and economic forces contributed to FDI liberalization. As developing countries democratized policy makers grew more attentive to the economic policy preferences of labor as its support was more necessary for political survival. At the same time, technological advances and growing trade liberalization prompted more MNCs to reorganize their production across multiple countries to leverage lower production costs. Previously, most firms used FDI as a way to compete in foreign product markets. Export-oriented FDI creates fewer costs for local producers because it does raise competition for consumers. Thus, local firms' incentives to lobby for protection grew weaker for industries in which export-oriented investments dominated, typically manufacturing industries.

Three sets of empirical analyses test a broad range of this theory's observable implications. Chapter 4 confirms that individual FDI preferences, as revealed in public opinion surveys, are consistent with my theory of FDI's distributive effects. Survey respondents who stand to gain the most from unrestricted FDI are the most likely to express support for it. Further, this analysis controls for several alternate economic and noneconomic explanations of FDI preferences. Original data on foreign-ownership restrictions covering the period 1970–2000 makes it possible for the first time to illustrate and analyze country and industry-level variation in the frequency of formal FDI entry barriers. In Chapter 5 I use these data to show that, on average, democracies impose foreign ownership restrictions on fewer industries than do non-democracies. A battery of robustness tests accounts for other possible explanations, possible measurements concerns, and alternate model specifications. Chapter 6 turns to cross-industry variation, specifically, the sharp decline of foreign-ownership barriers in manufacturing relative to modest and mixed changes in services industries. In analyzing the frequency of ownership restrictions in 2000, I find that simultaneous to vigorous competition for FDI, countries continued to limit foreign ownership in industries that receive market-oriented investments, typically services industries. This finding holds when account is taken of fine-grained industry features that mediate FDI's distributive effects.

This research not only resolves long-standing contradictions about the politics of FDI, but it reveals news insights about FDI's role in larger aspects of international economic integration. With regard to global production networks, it shows how a particular subset of such networks, production fragmented across countries but within a single firm, emerged. This subset grew, and ushered in a new era of openness to FDI, precisely because it was production for export rather than to compete for customers in the host countries' market. These networks flourished because opposition to liberalizing FDI into these industries was less.

Further, this research identifies FDI's role in the creation of a global market for services. Almost by definition services cannot be traded at arm's length; services are produced and consumed simultaneously and typically require close physical proximity. While a small portion of services can be traded at arm's length due to technological advances, such as back-office operations like call centers, most services remain nontradable. FDI in services is one of the few conduits for international market pressures in traditionally nontraded sectors. Local firms must contend with more efficient foreign competitors operating in their local markets. As I discuss in this chapter, FDI in services is particularly controversial because of entry barriers that countries continue to erect to prevent MNC entry into those industries.

7.1 Advancing FDI Research

This book has shown the need to open up the "black box of FDI" by paying closer attention to firms' motives and specific economic activities. Beyond their shared exceptional productivity, MNCs vary widely in the sources of their productivity advantages and how they capitalize on their productivity. Researchers can neither see nor explain this variation so long as their theories continue to rely on highly stylized priors about the motives for FDI or their empirical tests rely on aggregate estimates of FDI's monetary value.

By attending to variation in MNCs' motives and activities, scholars can more accurately specify both demand and supply-side theories for the political economy of FDI. For example, in Chapter 2 I contrasted market-export and export-oriented motives as a key source of variation in FDI's distributive effects under the period of study. More recent FDI flows, however, have an entirely different source. In the late 1980s, there arose international markets for venture capital and private equity. Professional money managers make high-risk, large-scale equity investments in new or underperforming firms in order to sell their shares at a profit within a fixed timeframe of about a decade.

Standard balance of payment estimates group production- and finance-oriented FDI, even though they bear little resemblance to one another. Accordingly, we should expect these types of investors to respond to host country political conditions in different ways. For instance, standard theories of political risk strongly emphasize MNCs' concerns about property-rights protections in host countries. This emphasis makes sense for the stylized production-oriented FDI that existing models assume. Property-rights protections, however, likely matter less to a foreign venture capital investor, because that investor tolerates more risk, given the inherent risks in venture capital investment, and because legal enforcement is less effective, given the relatively inchoate nature of much of the property at stake in these investments.

Additionally, focused theories of FDI more readily reveal the political economy implications of FDI's links to other aspects of international economic integration. For example, consider how trade agreements influence the incentives to engage in FDI. Current research emphasizes that trade agreements should stimulate FDI inflows, because they are credible commitments to economic openness (Büthe and Milner 2008), or because, under some circumstances, they confer privileged market access to certain firms (Chase 2003; Tobin and Busch 2010). Unpacking FDI by investors' motives reveals the many other ways in which investors' might react to trade agreements. When countries commit more to free trade, they weaken MNCs' incentives to engage in market-oriented FDI for the production and sale of products that can be traded across borders. Alternately, trade agreements can increase private equity investments as firms and industries adjust to higher scale economies that larger markets provide. Existing theories do not distinguish between these mechanisms, and empirical tests that rely on balance-of-payments FDI estimates can only capture the net effect of these opposing mechanisms. With a detailed understanding of FDI, researchers can more accurately infer how trade agreements have affected FDI inflows.

Variation in investment objectives is only one of many ways in which to parse FDI as a form of economic activity. Other potentially salient dimensions of variation include the mode of investment – establishing a new firm or acquiring a previously existing firm, sourcing decisions – importing production inputs or acquiring them from local suppliers, and specific types of firm-specific assets – patented production technologies, extensive distribution networks, and consumer brand recognition. By paying attention to these aspects of FDI political economy scholars can draw on the extensive theoretical innovations in trade economics that link trade and FDI to firm-level attributes (Melitz 2003, Helpman 2006).

These theoretical advances require correspondingly better measures and data, particularly firm-level data. Measuring FDI as international equity investment in excess of 10 percent is now too blunt a measure for FDI research. In the public domain alone, firm-level information includes stock market performance, annual reports, legally mandated financial reports, and intellectual property such as trademark and patent filings. Scholars can also access private financial databases with historical data on all manner of firm activities. When necessary, scholars can aggregate these firm-level data to calculate insightful industry-level summary statistics (e.g. mean, variance).

These suggestions for further FDI research speak to a larger research program on the political economy of international production that this book advances. Trade and FDI are inextricably linked, as complements in export-oriented investment, or as substitutes in market-oriented investments. With few exceptions however, political economy theories treat trade and FDI in isolation. By shifting toward the microlevel analysis of international production, researchers must pay attention to firms' linked decisions about trade and FDI and to how politics systematically influences firm behavior.

A unified approach to the political economy of international production highlights how the precise content of firms' production activities is politically salient. Current research focuses on the quality of host country contracting institutions in firms' choice to internalize their global production via FDI (Antràs 2003, Bernard, Jensen, Redding, and Schott 2010). When we consider firms' activities in more detail, policies and institutions can have a much larger role in guiding this choice (Antràs and Helpman 2008). For instance, to the extent that segments of production processes require highly specialized human capital, social insurance policies that encourage investment in specialized skills are a source of comparative advantage in attracting export-oriented FDI in industries that require such skills. A variety of other firm characteristics can shape the role of politics in firm behavior including a firm's relative productivity, size of plant-level scale economies, number of product varieties, and the volatility of product demand. Among other insights, greater attention to the content of production may reveal nonlinear relationships between MNC behavior and host country political risk.

Additionally, this unified approach to international production identifies how future exogenous change in the ease of fragmenting production alters the distributive consequences of market integration. In Chapter 2, I described how declining transport and communication costs contributed to the rise of export-oriented FDI in the last decades of the twentieth century. In much the same way, future technological change promises to trigger further reorganization of production across borders. One likely source of technological change is the automation of routine and codifiable production tasks through computing technology (Autor, Levy, and Murnane 2003). Through greater automation the composition of remaining MNCs' production tasks will be more heavily weighted towards complex, communication-intensive tasks that cannot be readily automated. This should be particularly true of service industry MNCs that are more likely to require direct communication with host country consumers (Oldenski 2012). At the margins, we can expect a corresponding change in the type of host country human capital that MNCs employ. MNCs will demand more labor capable of non-routine, communication-intensive tasks in the host country. To the extent that automation replaces the tasks of skilled host country labor there could a relative decline in MNC demand for skilled labor.

7.2 FDI and the Twenty-First-Century-Global Economy

A solid command of FDI's distributive consequences not only advances scholarly research, but also helps to anticipate future political controversies about FDI's role in the international economy. Given the dramatic decline in national foreign ownership regulations, some might be tempted to conclude that FDI regulation is a historical relic. Indeed, at the end of the twentieth century the most prominent controversies about FDI centered on a proverbial race to the bottom, in essence a concern about countries' excessive FDI openness. Average foreign-ownership restrictions remain low, and the growing frequency of investment clauses in preferential trade agreements anchors countries' openness in legally-binding treaties.

Such a conclusion about FDI is, at best, highly premature. Although widespread dramatic spikes in foreign-ownership regulations are unlikely in the foreseeable future, there are still vigorous debates within countries about the virtues of FDI openness and conflicts between countries over the scope of MNCs' market access. Although the exact points of contention may be different, they are, for the most part, new manifestations of the same underlying distributive conflicts that I have described in this book.

Perhaps the defining characteristic of the early twenty-first century global economy is the emergence of large, rapidly growing economies like China, India, and Brazil. Though some of the world's most populous countries, until the end of the twentieth century, they were conspicuously absent from international product and capital markets, because of their decades-long pursuits of state-led industrialization. Their opening to the international economy has both contributed to their remarkable growth and heighted tensions with their advanced industrialized counterparts.

In this section, I examine FDI's role in three specific aspects of this dynamic: the growing prominence of emerging markets, disputes over MNCs' access to emerging markets, and controversies over emerging market-based MNCs' access to industrialized countries' markets. Here, I highlight continuing political debates about FDI's distributive effects that are in many respects a continuation of twentieth-century controversies.

To varying degrees, FDI inflows fueled the growth of these large developing economies. Consider the case of China. China initially opened to FDI with a 1979 law that permitted FDI through joint ventures with state-owned Chinese firms. Communist Party Chairman Deng Xiaoping, justifying this limited opening, quipped, "In joint ventures with foreigners, 50 percent still belongs to socialism" (Pearson 1991, 102). These foreign-ownership restrictions were of the standard variety, designed to force technology transfer from MNCs to state-owned firms.[1]

China did not become a leading destination for FDI until well into the 1990s, after it liberalized ownership for export-oriented investments through the creation of four special economic zones (SEZs) in coastal provinces. MNCs that operate in China's SEZs received special dispensation from strict labor laws and a measure of autonomy that was previously unknown to foreign firms operating in China. Following the 1989 student protests in Tiananmen Square, Chinese leaders further liberalized foreign ownership to compensate for investors' concerns about China's political instability. FDI inflows also accelerated in anticipation of China's entry into the WTO (Branstetter and Lardy 2006).

At first glance it may seem that China poses a challenge to my claim that democratization contributed to FDI liberalization: China is not a democracy, but it has become a leading destination for FDI. In fact, China's experience is consistent with this book's key findings. China's extensive use of foreign-ownership restrictions is consistent with the book's finding that autocrats tend to restrict ownership for the benefit of local firms. China opened to export-oriented FDI but has continued to protect industries in which FDI would compete with local firms (Branstetter and Feenstra 2002). China also demonstrates the gains to labor from unrestricted FDI. When foreign-invested firms were free of Chinese labor regulations they paid higher wages to encourage productivity, and foreign and domestic firms competed vigorously for skilled workers.

What do my findings portend about the future role of FDI politics in the growth of emerging markets? For emerging markets like China that have experienced FDI-fueled growth, the challenge to sustaining that growth lies

---

[1] Joint-venture regulations specified several requirements designed to secure Chinese managerial control. For example local Chinese partners were heads of state-owned enterprises and typically Communist Party members. Corporate governance rules raised Chinese partners' de facto control by granting exceptional oversight to appointed boards of directors, requiring that the board chair be Chinese, and requiring that all board decisions be approved by unanimous vote. By law all personnel matters remained exclusively under Chinese control (Gallagher 2007).

in attracting more sophisticated export-oriented FDI that maximizes the potential for productivity spillovers to local firms. This requires countries to provide the more robust property rights protections needed to entice the most productive MNCs to introduce their most valuable firm-specific assets. Further, countries will have to reinforce their capacity to absorb these productivity spillovers by expanding the stock of human capital and accelerating financial development. Otherwise high growth emerging markets like India that underperform in attracting FDI will need to address deficiencies in basic infrastructure and unwieldy market regulations. The flip side of these challenges in sustaining growth is the expansion of FDI-fueled growth to additional emerging markets. For instance, rising labor costs in China are prompting MNCs to locate subsidiaries in lower cost markets in the region like Vietnam.

FDI also promises to be a source of conflict between emerging and advanced economies. On both sides of this relationship there are disputes over MNCs' market access. These conflicts illustrate why the distinction between export- and market-oriented FDI continues to grow more politically salient. While most countries have embraced export-oriented FDI inflows, market-oriented investments continue to pose direct threats to the profits of local producers. Market access disputes are, for the time being, more likely in these service sectors due to the lack of a comprehensive multilateral regime governing trade in services. The WTO's General Agreement on Trade in Services specifically identifies FDI as a form of "trade" in nontradable services sectors, but the limited scope of that agreement creates few binding requirements on member countries.

The world's advanced industrialized economies balk at the FDI entry barriers that their MNCs encounter in emerging markets. Indeed, the prosperity of emerging markets actually magnifies tensions, because it makes their domestic markets more attractive to foreign MNCs. Tensions over FDI market access increasingly dominate bilateral trade disputes. In recent years, the U.S. Trade Representative has raised concerns about U.S. firms' access to the Chinese markets for electronic payments, audio-visual services, and electricity services. In several advanced countries, retailers have been pushing their governments to pressure India to liberalize foreign-ownership restrictions on multi-product retailers. Wal-Mart alone spent U.S.$25 million over four years to lobby U.S. lawmakers to help the firm enter the Indian market.[2] MNCs seeking to invest in Brazil face entry barriers into the finance

---

[2]   Prasanta Sahu and Rumman Ahmed, "India Assures Wal-Mart on FDI Policy," *Wall Street Journal* Jan. 25, 2013. Online at http://online.wsj.com/article/SB10001424127887323539804578261522732301016.html#articleTabs%3Darticle (accessed January 25, 2013).

sector among other industries. That the United States finds itself in conflict with China, India, and Brazil is no surprise, because these are among the largest consumer markets in the world.

Contingent on the sustained prosperity of the large emerging markets, conflicts over MNCs' market access will likely intensify. Preferential trade agreements can address these conflicts by continuing to embed FDI liberalization provisions. In order for multilateral cooperation to successfully address this conflict, agreements must codify the liberalization of services FDI as a mode of trade in services. While meaningful trade in services liberalization has proven intractable the growing market potential of the emerging economies could be sufficient to break the logjam.

A new point of conflict in the international economy is the growing prominence of emerging market-based MNCs and their access to the domestic markets of advanced industrialized countries.[3] The growth of FDI originating from emerging markets is another reflection of emerging markets' prosperity. Emerging market MNCs often acquire foreign firms to expand their portfolio of firm-specific assets including production technologies and consumer brands and gain a foothold in the host market. Recent high-profile acquisitions including the Brazilian firm InBev's purchase of the U.S. firm Anheuser Busch, and India's Tata Corporation's purchase of Britain's Land Rover and Jaguar.

In advanced industrialized countries opponents of these investments cite national security concerns, echoing the earliest FDI regulations described in Chapter 1. Following the terrorist attacks of September 11, 2001, a profound shift in attitudes about natural security threats have put FDI under renewed political scrutiny in the United States. For example, in 2006, Dubai Ports World, a shipping and logistics company owned by a Dubai government agency, sought to acquire P&O Navigation Company, a British firm that had long managed several major ports along the east coast of the United States. The Committee on Foreign Investment in the United States (CFIUS), the executive agency committee charged with national security review of proposed foreign acquisitions, approved the deal. Nonetheless, the proposal generated sharp Congressional opposition. New Jersey senator Frank Lautenberg declared, "Don't let them tell you this is just the transfer of title. Baloney. We wouldn't transfer title to the Devil; we're not going to transfer title to Dubai" (Graham and Marchick 2006,136).

The recent politicization of FDI has been framed as a matter of national security. Yet, distributive concerns remain a durable rival explanation for

---

[3]   See Sauvant (2009) for a description of these trends worldwide.

FDI's politics. In the Dubai Ports World case, national security rhetoric masked the efforts of a single American firm that stood to lose from the transaction. Eller and Company, a small, Miami, Florida-based stevedoring firm wanted to block the transaction to gain leverage in a long-standing unrelated dispute with P&O. Eller failed to convince CFIUS to block the deal, but then lobbied Congress to intervene. The spokesman for New York senator Charles Schumer, the most prominent Congressional critic of the proposed deal, described Eller as "the canary in the mineshaft for many people on the Hill" (Graham and Marchick 2006,139).[4] In practice it is difficult to parse national security and distributional explanations – both were likely present – and national security concerns arise in only a small fraction of investments. Nonetheless, future calls for FDI regulation may invoke national security to mask efforts to protect domestic firms from foreign MNCs.

The scope for future conflict over emerging market FDI into advanced economies depends in part on patterns of development and growth in the emerging markets. Natural resources and infrastructure will continue to be controversial but acquisitions in manufacturing will wane if emerging market MNCs develop sufficient independent technical expertise and brand recognition. Particularly successful country-industries may even engage in less controversial greenfield investments. The experience of Japanese automobile MNCs in the U.S. provides a useful analogy. Advanced country consumers should also grow more accepting of these firms' products as being of sufficient quality.[5]

The evolution of the world economy is sure to produce dramatic and unexpected changes in the content and organization of economic activity and political representation. This book provides a detailed analysis of FDI regulation that can continue to anchor our thinking about the politics of FDI and its pivotal and evolving role in the world economy.

---

[4] There are similar examples prior to the September 11 attacks. The United States is among the most open economies in the world to FDI and although the CFIUS mandate is narrow, there are numerous examples of firms with clear commercial motives lobbying the committee to block specific acquisitions. In 1990, 119 members of Congress requested review of British Tire and Rubber's proposed hostile takeover of the Norton Company, a Massachusetts-based company. The letter expressed concern that the proposed takeover would be inimical to U.S. national security. After Norton received a more lucrative offer from a French company, the objections were abruptly withdrawn (Graham and Marchick 2006).

[5] See Verelegh and Steenkamp 1999 on product country of origin and consumer demand.

APPENDIX

Existing and New Measures of FDI Regulation

This appendix describes FDI regulatory instruments and how they are measured. The first section describes substantive dimensions of FDI regulation including the specific policies that countries have used and the different ways in which countries set these policies. The second section addresses the measurement of FDI regulation. I review existing proxies of FDI regulation and describe the creation of the original FDI regulations data used in this book.

A1. Instruments of FDI Regulation: Types and Sources

A1.1 FDI Regulatory Instruments

Countries use a variety of policy instruments to regulate FDI. Although these policies vary in their precise distributive effects, the underlying motive for their use is the same: to redistribute assets and/or the income they generate from MNCs to parties in the host country. There are two classes of FDI regulation: entry barriers and post-entry regulation. In Chapter 3 I described entry barriers in some detail. To summarize that discussion, entry barriers are policies that restrict the terms under which foreigners can make direct investments. Ownership restrictions limit the percent equity that foreigners may hold and typically require the foreigner to be a minority (e.g., less than 49 percent) shareholder in what is in essence a forced joint venture. The effect of involuntary mandatory joint ventures is to dampen the potential positive effects of FDI by making investing firms less likely to transfer their latest technologies and keep jointly owned affiliates less integrated with the parent company, further cutting back on the desired beneficial technology transfer (Ramachandran 1993, Knickerbocker 1973, Henisz and Williamson 2000). Affiliates that are joint ventures are also less likely to be integrated into global production networks, further reducing the spillovers. Available evidence on backward linkages indicates that backward productivity spillovers are more likely when affiliates are wholly foreign owned (Moran 1998).

Screening requirements mandate that all proposed foreign investments undergo review by a public regulatory body that has full discretion to reject individual proposed investments.[1] Screening is typically conducted by a standing investment review body organized under the auspices of the central bank, treasury, or commerce ministry; ad hoc bodies assembled to review particular projects; or a decentralized approval process in which potential investors have to obtain approvals from multiple regulatory bodies. Also included in this category are those industries in which only foreign investors, and not their domestic counterparts, must obtain a license in order to operate in the industry. This mechanism can be used to selectively protect industries from foreign competition on an ad hoc basis (Encarnation and Wells 1985).

Countries also regulate the activities of foreign-owned firms after their entry into the market. These are regulations that apply only to foreign-owned firms. Otherwise identical domestic firms are not subject to these policies. Performance requirements are policies that govern MNCs production practices. Local sourcing requirements, also referred to as domestic content requirements, require foreign-owned firms to obtain a specified portion of their production inputs from suppliers within the host country. The stated purpose of this type of provision is to generate demand for production inputs produced by domestic firms. Virtually all studies of the income effects of these requirements find that they are welfare reducing because they force producers to pay higher than world prices for production inputs, resulting in higher product prices (Moran 1998). The suboptimal scale of local inputs producers is the main reason for this effect. Local content requirements also slow technology transfer for the same reason described earlier with regard to mandatory joint venture requirements.

Mandatory export requirements require investing firms to export a certain percent of their production output out of the host country. The benefits to the host country include an improvement in the balance of payments of

---

[1] Countries can also use the screening process to ascertain whether a project is eligible for certain investment incentives. This variable does not include optional screening to determine a project's eligibility for various incentives provided by the host country or pro forma registration requirements.

the country and reduced output for sale in the local market. Moran (1998) argues that export requirements are actually welfare increasing for those countries that are large enough and have sufficiently low production costs, because these countries give investing firms a unique incentive to make initial export-oriented investment where they would not do so otherwise because of the relative lack of information regarding the local market. For these positive welfare effects to be sustained, they usually have to be reinforced with substantial investment incentives and extensive export promotion by the host country (the costs of which generate their own set of distributional effects). Mandatory export requirements are likely to deter investors primarily interested in serving the local market.

Another set of regulations governs MNCs' financial and corporate activities.

Discriminatory tax treatment for foreign-owned firms subjects these firms to higher tax rates than local firms. The stated purpose of such policies is simply to extract more of the profits of the foreign-owned firms. Generally, such tax provisions are rare, most likely because such discrimination would encourage investing firms to evade taxes through their transfer pricing of goods between the parent and subsidiary firms. Analyses of the determinants of FDI flows have mixed results on the influence of tax policies on FDI inflows. Although empirical findings are not conclusive, tax policies do not appear to have a large effect on FDI inflows (Hines 1995, Wheeler and Mody 1992).

Capital repatriation provisions limit the percent of total profits or assets that MNCs may repatriate, or specify a mandatory waiting period during which time the country prohibits repatriation. For example, in the 1970s, many Latin American countries limited profit repatriation to between 10 percent and 20 percent of the total value of investment over a three- to five-year period. Another variant of this policy taxes capital outflows. The desired effect of these limits is to encourage foreign-owned firms to reinvest profits within the country. These provisions may reduce FDI inflows by effectively rendering investments less liquid, although in practice, it is not as large a barrier to restrictions because companies often choose to reinvest earnings in the local market rather than repatriating profits.

Some countries limit MNCs' access to foreign exchange. This limit may be an explicit limit or a specification of a different, less favorable rate at which foreign-owned firms can convert capital. Such limits make it less advantageous for foreign-owned firms to repatriate profits or acquire production inputs abroad. The distributional effects of this policy are similar to those of capital control as its ultimate effect is to make foreign-owned firms marginally more credit constrained.

Local employment requirements mandate that a specified percentage of a foreign-owned firm's labor force must be host country nationals. In most cases these data refer to total employment, but there are some instances when minimums apply only to managers. This policy is akin to a specific type of local content requirement; host countries use this policy to increase technological and human capital spillovers. Distortions created by these policies are likely to be small because FDI, almost by definition, relies on local labor. Labor minimums specifically for managers are likely to have a larger effect because these are positions for which MNCs tend to use expatriate managers who possess firm-specific knowledge that complements invested capital assets. A related policy stipulates that a certain percentage of foreign firms' boards of directors be nationals of the host country. The precise welfare and distributional effects depend on hosts' corporate governance rules and how nationality influences voting behavior within firms.

FDI regulations are mostly national policies. The legal form of regulations varies widely, ranging from administrative regulations to national laws and even constitutional prohibitions on foreign ownership. Since the late 1990s, preferential trade agreements increasingly have investment liberalization provisions that extend the concept of most favored nation status to the FDI context.[2] For example, Chapter 11 of the North American Free Trade Agreement (NAFTA) requires member countries to extend most-favored-nation (MFN) status to firms based in other NAFTA countries. Bilateral investment treaties have limited implications for FDI restrictions. These treaties emphasize dispute settlement procedures and tax harmonization rather than market access issues. Countries may codify existing national regulations into the treaties, but there are no negotiations on market access.

Multilateral efforts to liberalize FDI inflows have had limited success. In 1997, the Organization for Economic Cooperation and Development (OECD) proposed the Multilateral Agreement on Investment, a far-reaching

---

[2] The Andean Pact is an early example of a regional economic agreement that included restrictions on FDI. These included restrictions on ownership, local content requirements, and scheduled transfers of ownership from MNCs to local firms. In the 1970s, many developing counties called for voluntary codes on FDI regulation that would grant them more authority to expropriate MNC assets than was allowed under customary international law. See Krasner (1985, chapter 7). More generally, earlier international agreements relevant to FDI were often voluntary coordination devices established under the auspices of the OECD or the United Nations (Keohane and Van Ooms 1975).

treaty that would have required countries to phase out national FDI regulations. The proposal drew the ire of civil society groups concerned about FDI's consequences for human rights, labor standards, and the environment. A year later the OECD abandoned the proposal in response to these protests. Two World Trade Organization (WTO) agreements deal with FDI regulation. The 1996 Agreement on Trade-Related Investment Measures bans the use of performance requirements as indirect trade barriers. The 1995 General Agreement on Trade in Services allowed countries to make voluntary commitments to liberalize foreign ownership in services sectors such as telecommunications and finance.

Local and regional policies can also influence the ease with which MNCs invest. There are examples of local municipalities that regulate the entry of foreign-owned firms into the provision of urban public services like water, power, and sewage. Typically, however, subnational policy makers are more active in policies to attract investment rather than limiting investment. Often there is competition among subnational units to attract investors to one jurisdiction over another. Some countries grant subnational policy makers wide latitude. Starting in the 1980s, China devolved much of its FDI regulation to provinces and localities that in turn leveraged it into more investment through laxer regulation (Gallagher 2007).

A1.2 Measuring FDI Regulation

Existing metrics of FDI regulations suffer from at least one of three limitations. First, these proxies are almost entirely national-level aggregate measures that do not distinguish between industries.[3] These data preclude consideration of any industry-level variation in FDI policies. Second, most measures rely on indirect evidence of FDI regulations that conflate formal policies with political risk to foreign investors or countries' overall regulatory climate. Third, existing measures have limited historical coverage dating back to only the mid-1980s. For example, Political Risk Services' *International Country Risk Guide*, a standard source for investment risk data, begins in 1984. This section describes these existing measures and how they compare to the original data used in this book.

The most prominent of existing proxies for FDI regulation are business climate indicators. These measures aggregate indicators of countries' formal openness and informal "receptiveness" to economic activity by summarizing

[3] Hardin and Holmes (2000) and Golub (2003) are exceptions.

a variety of economic, social, and political factors that influence the profitability of foreign investment projects, including corruption, administrative burdens, and political stability. Many of the indicators rely on investor surveys to gauge the investment climate. Some of these measures are specific to foreign investors, including Political Risk Services' *International Country Risk Guide*, Business Environment Risk Intelligence's (BERI) Business Risk Service, World Economic Forum's *World Competitiveness Yearbook*, Economist Intelligence Unit, and Pricewaterhouse Coopers' *Doing Business and Investment* series. Two common metrics, the *Wall Street Journal/* Heritage Foundation's Index of Economic Freedom and the World Bank's *Doing Business* indicators (Dollar, Hallward-Driemeier, and Mengistae 2006), approximate overall regulatory barriers to economic activity, not just those specific to foreign investors.

Business climate measures are poor proxies for FDI regulations because they conflate formal restrictions with a variety of other country characteristics that are not explicit policy choices. Survey-based measures suffer from a number of methodological shortcomings including selection bias in the survey sample stemming from the need to survey those with sufficient knowledge of individual cases to make an assessment (Henisz 2000). For example, surveys of foreign managers operating in a country necessarily selects for those firms who found the local market attractive enough to invest. Although investment climate surveys enjoy wide use as general proxies of investment attitudes, they are noisy measures of policy outcomes.

Another common approach utilizes International Monetary Fund (IMF) data on capital account restrictions to proxy for FDI regulation. These data are deployed to test hypotheses that do not distinguish between FDI and portfolio capital flows (Johnston et al. 1999, Quinn and Inclán 1997). This approach rests on the assumption that multinational firms and holders of portfolio capital respond similarly to capital controls, an assumption that is difficult to support in light of the different objectives of these two types of international investment. A variant of this strategy acknowledges the uniqueness of FDI and makes use of FDI-specific components of these IMF data that indicate if MNCs face restrictions on their FDI-related capital movements like the remittance of profits out of the host country (Schindler 2009, Alfaro 2004). This represents a commendable effort to utilize FDI-specific data, but these data measure the presence of only one type of FDI restriction – limits on the movement of liquid capital flows, like subsidiaries' profits, in connection with FDI. Not only are data for this single type of restriction not a good summary measure of FDI restrictions, but in practice they may not even pose a barrier to FDI. MNCs can evade formal capital controls with relative ease by manipulating the valuation of inputs and investments between a firm's headquarters and subsidiaries. The existence of such policies conveys useful information about countries' intent to regulate, but the actual effects of these targeted capital controls may be limited. A somewhat related measure derives from UNCTAD reviews of investment policies. In its annual publication *World Investment Report*, the organization reports two measures: the number of FDI-related policy changes that are liberalizing and the number of changes that are restricting in a given year. They do not publish country values, much less values for specific policies in each country, but for present purposes the major short-coming of these data are that they group together several types of policies including those specifically targeted at MNCs and other forms of regulation that, although relevant for MNCs, cannot be interpreted as a measure to restrict investment.

More recently, scholars have turned to gravity models to derive esti-mates of the cumulative effect of national policies and characteristics on FDI inflows. Gravity models begin with a theoretical model of FDI deter-minants that is used to predict FDI flows. For example, UNCTAD's (2003) Inward FDI Potential Index calculates predicted FDI inflows based on eight measures of host market potential and investment climate. These theo-retical estimates are then compared with actual FDI flows data, with any gap between them for a given country attributed to that country's general attitude toward FDI inflows, either positive or negative depending on the direction of the gap. Although the development of FDI gravity models is still in the early stages, the poor quality of FDI flow data is a strong rea-son to be circumspect about these efforts. MNCs develop internal capital markets entirely within the firm, usually a complex system of borrowing and lending activities between headquarters and various subsidiaries. Over time, MNCs have come to rely more heavily on internal capital markets. For example, in the 1990s, roughly 60 percent of total capital flows from U.S.-based MNCs to their foreign affiliates was in the form of reinvested profits previously generated in the same subsidiary (Mataloni 1995).[4] These capital flows never appear in national balance-of-payments statistics, the source for FDI flow data used in gravity model estimates. To the extent that under-lying FDI flow data misrepresents the true extent of investment activity, any derivative policy estimates need to be interpreted with a great deal of cau-tion. Additionally, if MNCs' financing patterns, especially their propensity

---

[4] Knickerbocker (1973) documents a similar propensity in the 1960s of MNCs reinvesting subsidiary profits.

to use financing methods that appear in balance-of-payments data, vary with host country characteristics that also influence the decision to invest, results may be biased. Desai et al. (2004) find that MNCs' decision to utilize internal capital markets varies systematically with host country's conditions, including the depth of capital markets and creditor rights. Estimates for those variables that are associated with both the decision to invest and the form of financing will be biased upward.

Some of the more promising of the existing measures take inspiration from the coverage ratio measures developed to study nontariff barriers (NTB) to trade in goods. Coverage ratios measure the percent of total imports, measured in quantity or price value, which is subject to a specific type of NTB (Deardorff and Stern 1998). The patterning of FDI policy data after NTB measures is methodologically appealing because it can be used to generate industry-specific measures. For example, Hardin and Holmes (2000) calculate tariff equivalents of FDI restrictions in Asian service sectors. Golub (2003) generates industry-level estimates for a sample of OECD countries by weighting different regulatory barriers into a single index of FDI restriction. These examples, however, rely on FDI inflows disaggregated by industries that are unavailable outside of a handful of countries. As the collection of FDI data becomes more systematic and detailed, as it promises to in the coming years, this will be a promising avenue for developing new FDI policy measures.

In sum, existing proxies for FDI policies are generally appropriate for the studies in which they are deployed but are insufficient to examine the sources of FDI regulation.

Original Dataset of FDI Regulations

The main source for these data is *Overseas Business Reports,* a U.S. Commerce Department publication series that provides detailed summaries of individual countries' economic policies and market profiles to assist Americans engaged in commercial activities abroad. After 1993, this publication was discontinued and replaced by *US Country Commercial Guides,* another U.S. Commerce Department publication from which I obtained the 1993–2000 data. These publications are quite comparable, but there are some minor differences. The Commerce Department's in-house country experts compiled *Overseas Business Reports* whereas U.S. embassy staffs produce *US Country Commercial Guides.* The format of *US Country Commercial Guides* is standardized whereas *Overseas Business Reports* are somewhat less standardized and some, usually smaller, countries are treated infrequently. Because

of the less frequent publication of *Overseas Business Reports* beginning in
the early 1980s, the 1985–2000 period is supplemented with data coded
from the annual *National Trade Barrier Estimate Report*, an annual reporting to the U.S. Congress of foreign trade and investment barriers required
under the 1983 U.S. Trade Act.

Each observation in the raw data is at the industry-country-year level.
For the data used to calculate *Entry Restrictions*, the variable analyzed in
Chapters 2 and 5, and *Restriction Counts*, the variable featured in Chapter 6,
the disaggregate measure equals 1 if there is a restriction on foreign ownership and 0 otherwise. A binary measure is most appropriate because ownership regulations usually stipulate that majority ownership – that is, greater
than 50 percent – must be held in local hands. Often countries do not specify a specific percentage and when they do, it is almost always a 49 percent
limit on foreign ownership.

The country coverage of the dataset is a function of which countries
appeared in these publications. There are more than 100 countries in the
dataset, so there is little reason to be concerned that the sample is systematically biased. The one major omission is of (former) Soviet bloc countries.
The data sources only began reporting data for these countries in the last
few years of the sample. Table A1 provides a list of all countries in the dataset classified by region.

In coding the data, I selected the most appropriate industry classification
from the International Standard Industrial Classification (ISIC) Revision
3, the United Nation's official classification for economic activity.[5] I choose
Revision 3 because it includes the most accurate classifications for current
economic activities; older versions of the classification do not include as
much fine detail about more recent forms of economic activity. Table A2
lists the two-digit ISIC Rev 3 categories to provide a sense of how the classification scheme is organized.

I coded the raw data at the most appropriate industrial classification,
ranging from one- to four-digit aggregations. For example, I code a ban
on foreign ownership in transportation as a ban on foreign ownership in
three two-digit categories: land transport (ISIC 6000), water transport

---

[5] Because of the ISIC scheme, it is sometimes necessary to classify restrictions at a higher
level of aggregation than would be preferred. For example, countries often subject investment in domestic air transport to a different set of regulations than international air
transport. The air transportation category (ISIC 6200), however, is only divided into two
subcategories: "scheduled air transport" (ISIC 6210) and "nonscheduled air transport"
(ISIC 6220). In this case, an FDI restriction in domestic air transport is coded at the more
aggregate (ISIC 6200) level.

Table A1 *Countries in dataset, by region*

Africa	Asia	Europe/ Canada	Middle East/ North Africa	Latin America/ Caribbean
Botswana	Afghanistan	Austria	Algeria	Argentina
Burkina Faso	Australia	Belgium	Bahrain	Bolivia
Cameroon	Bangladesh	Canada	Egypt	Brazil
Chad	China	Cyprus	Iran	Chile
Cote d'Ivoire	Fiji	Denmark	Israel	Colombia
Eritrea	India	Finland	Jordan	Costa Rica
Gabon	Indonesia	France	Kenya	Dominican Republic
Ghana	Japan	Germany	Kuwait	Ecuador
Guinea	Korea	Greece	Libya	El Salvador
Guinea Bissau	Malaysia	Ireland	Morocco	Guatemala
Lesotho	Myanmar	Italy	Oman	Guyana
Liberia	Nepal	Netherlands	Qatar	Haiti
Madagascar	New Zealand	Norway	Saudi Arabia	Honduras
Malawi	Papua New Guinea	Portugal	Turkey	Jamaica
Mauritania	Pakistan	Switzerland	Tunisia	Mexico
Mauritius	Philippines	Spain	UAE	Nicaragua
Mozambique	Singapore	United Kingdom	Yemen	Panama
Namibia	Sri Lanka			Paraguay
Niger	Thailand			Peru
Nigeria	Vietnam			Trinidad & Tobago
Senegal				Venezuela
South Africa				Uruguay
Rwanda				
Sudan				
Sierra Leone				
Togo				
Swaziland				
Tanzania				
Uganda				
Zambia				
Zaire/Democratic Republic of Congo				

Table A2 *Industries in full FDI regulation dataset*

Data were coded according to the most appropriate industry category of International Standard Industrial Classification (ISIC), Revision 3.1. Reported here is the two-digit level of industry classification. Each ISIC 2-digit category is further subdivided into more detailed three- and four-digit categories. The summary data reported here are two-digit industry aggregates. This list omits ISIC categories 1–14, agriculture and natural resources, and ISIC categories 95–99: activities of private households, international organizations, and foreign diplomatic posts. "n.e.c." = not elsewhere classified

Manufacturing
15 Manufacture of food products and beverages
16 Manufacture of tobacco products
17 Manufacture of textiles
18 Manufacture of wearing apparel; dressing and dyeing of fur
19 Tanning and dressing of leather; manufacture of luggage, handbags, saddlery, harness, and footwear
20 Manufacture of wood and of products of wood and cork, except furniture; manufacture of articles of straw and plaiting materials
21 Manufacture of paper and paper products
22 Publishing, printing, and reproduction of recorded media
23 Manufacture of coke, refined petroleum products, and nuclear fuel
24 Manufacture of chemicals and chemical products
25 Manufacture of rubber and plastics products
26 Manufacture of other nonmetallic mineral products
27 Manufacture of basic metals
28 Manufacture of fabricated metal products, except machinery and equipment
29 Manufacture of machinery and equipment n.e.c.
30 Manufacture of office, accounting, and computing machinery
31 Manufacture of electrical machinery and apparatus n.e.c.
32 Manufacture of radio, television, and communication equipment and apparatus
33 Manufacture of medical, precision, and optical instruments, watches, and clocks
34 Manufacture of motor vehicles, trailers, and semi-trailers
35 Manufacture of other transport equipment
36 Manufacture of furniture; manufacturing n.e.c.
37 Recycling

Electricity, Gas, and Water Supply
40 Electricity, gas, steam, and hot water supply
41 Collection, purification, and distribution of water

Construction
45 Construction
Wholesale and Retail Trade; Repair of Motor Vehicles, Motorcycles, and Personal and Household Goods

(*continued*)

50 Sale, maintenance, and repair of motor vehicles and motorcycles; retail sale of automotive fuel
51 Wholesale trade and commission trade, except of motor vehicles and motorcycles
52 Retail trade, except of motor vehicles and motorcycles; repair of personal and household goods

Hotels and Restaurants
55 Hotels and restaurants

Transport, Storage, and Communications
60 Land transport; transport via pipelines
61 Water transport
62 Air transport
63 Supporting and auxiliary transport activities; activities of travel agencies
64 Post and telecommunications

Financial Intermediations
65 Financial intermediation, except insurance and pension funding
66 Insurance and pension funding, except compulsory social security
67 Activities auxiliary to financial intermediation
Real Estate, Renting, and Business Activities
70 Real estate activities
71 Renting of machinery and equipment without operator and of personal and household goods
72 Computer and related activities
73 Research and development
74 Other business activities

Public Administration and Defense; Compulsory Social Security
75 Public administration and defense; compulsory social security

Education
80 Education

Health and Social Work
85 Health and social work

Other Community, Social, and Personal Service Activities
90 Sewage and refuse disposal, sanitation, and similar activities
91 Activities of membership organizations n.e.c.
92 Recreational, cultural, and sporting activities
93 Other service activities

(ISIC 6100), and air transport (ISIC 6200). By contrast, a ban on foreign ownership in railroads is coded as a restriction in the three-digit subcategory of land transportation for railroads (ISIC 6010, rail transport). This dataset encompasses fifty-seven two-digit ISIC categories and their associated subcategories. To create the variable *Entry Restrictions* used in Chapters 2 and 5, I collapse industry categories to their most disaggregated form (mostly four-digit ISIC categories with some two- and three-digit categories) and assign restrictions recorded at higher levels of industry aggregation to their associated subcategories. For each country-year I remove the industries in which there was no employment or output as reported by the UN's Industrial Development Organization and calculate the percent of industries in which there is an ownership restriction in each country-year. *Investment Screening* is identical in its construction except that the raw measure is the presence of a mandatory screening requirement.

Bibliography

Adler, Emanuel. 1986. "Ideological 'Guerrillas' and the Quest for Technological Autonomy: Brazil's Domestic Computer Industry." *International Organization* 40 (3): 673–705. doi:10.1017/S0020818300027314.

Aguiar, Mark, and Gita Gopinath. 2005. "Fire-Sale Foreign Direct Investment and Liquidity Crises." *Review of Economics and Statistics* 87 (3): 439–452. doi:10.1162/0034653054638319.

Aitken, Brian, Ann Harrison, and Robert E. Lipsey. 1996. "Wages and Foreign Ownership: A Comparative Study of Mexico, Venezuela, and the United States." *Journal of International Economics* 40 (3–4): 345–371. doi:10.1016/0022-1996 (95)01410-1.

Aizenman, Joshua. 2005. "Opposition to FDI and Financial Shocks." *Journal of Development Economics* 77 (2): 467–476. doi:10.1016/j.jdeveco.2004.04.004.

Alfaro, Laura. 2004. "Capital Controls: A Political Economy Approach." *Review of International Economics* 12 (4): 571–590.

Alfaro, Laura, Areendam Chanda, Sebnem Kalemli-Ozcan, and Selin Sayek. 2004. "FDI and Economic Growth: The Role of Local Financial Markets." *Journal of International Economics* 64 (1): 89–112.

Alfaro, Laura, and Andrew Charlton. 2009. "Intra-Industry Foreign Direct Investment." *American Economic Review* 99 (5): 2096–2119. doi:10.1257/aer.99.5.2096.

Alfaro, Laura, and Maggie Xiaoyang Chen. 2012. "Surviving the Global Financial Crisis: Foreign Ownership and Establishment Performance." *American Economic Journal: Economic Policy* 4 (3): 30–55.

Amsden, Alice H., and Takashi Hikino. 1994. "Project Execution Capability, Organizational Know-how and Conglomerate Corporate Growth in Late Industrialization." *Industrial and Corporate Change* 3 (1): 111 –147. doi:10.1093/icc/3.1.111.

Antràs, Pol. 2003. "Firms, Contracts, and Trade Structure." *Quarterly Journal of Economics* 118(4): 1375–1418.

Antràs, Pol, and Elhanan Helpman. 2008. "Contractual Frictions and Global Sourcing." In *The Organization of Firms in a Global Economy*, Elhanan Helpman, Thierry Verdier, and Dalia Marin. Cambridge, MA: Harvard University Press.

Antràs, Pol, Mihir A. Desai, and C. Fritz Foley. 2009. "Multinational Firms, FDI Flows, and Imperfect Capital Markets." *Quarterly Journal of Economics* 124 (3): 1171–1219. doi:10.1162/qjec.2009.124.3.1171.

Arnold, Jens Matthias, and Beata S. Javorcik. 2009. "Gifted Kids or Pushy Parents? Foreign Direct Investment and Plant Productivity in Indonesia." *Journal of International Economics* 79 (1): 42–53. doi:10.1016/j.jinteco.2009.05.004.

Autor, David H., Frank Levy, and Richard J. Murnane. 2003. "The Skill Content of Recent Technological Change: An Empirical Exploration." *Quarterly Journal of Economics* 118(4): 1279–1333.

Bagwell, Kyle. 2007. "The Economic Analysis of Advertising," In *Handbook of Industrial Organization Volume 3*, ed. Mark Armstrong and Robert Porter, pp. 1701–1844. Amsterdam: North-Holland.

Baker, Andy. 2005. "Who Wants to Globalize? Consumer Tastes and Labor Markets in a Theory of Trade Policy Beliefs." *American Journal of Political Science* 49 (4): 924–938. doi:10.2307/3647706.

Baldwin, Robert E. 1985. *The Political Economy of U.S. Import Policy*. Cambridge, MA: MIT Press.

Balsvik, Ragnhild, and Stefanie A. Haller. 2011. "Foreign Firms and Host-Country Productivity: Does the Mode of Entry Matter?" *Oxford Economic Papers* 63 (1): 158–186. doi:10.1093/oep/gpq014.

Barba Navaretti, Giorgio, Daniele Checchi, and Alessandro Turrini. 2003. "Adjusting Labor Demand: Multinational Versus National Firms: A Cross-European Analysis." *Journal of the European Economic Association* 1 (2/3): 708–719.

Barba Navaretti, Giorgio, and Anna Falzoni. 2004. "Home Country Effects of Foreign Direct Investment." In *Multinational Firms in the World Economy*, ed. Giorgio Barba Navaretti and Anthony J. Venables, pp. 217–238. Princeton, NJ: Princeton University Press.

Barba Navaretti, Giorgio, and Anthony J. Venables. 2004. *Multinational Firms in the World Economy*. Princeton, NJ: Princeton University Press.

Barry, Frank G. 2004. "FDI and the Host Economy: A Case Study of Ireland." In *Multinational Firms in the World Economy*, ed. Giorgio Barba Navaretti and Anthony J. Venables, pp. 187–216. Princeton, NJ: Princeton University Press.

Batra, Raveendra N, and Rama Ramachandran. 1980. "Multinational Firms and the Theory of International Trade and Investment." *American Economic Review* 70 (3): 278–290.

Beamish, Paul W., and John C. Banks. 1987. "Equity Joint Ventures and the Theory of the Multinational Enterprise." *Journal of International Business Studies* 18 (2): 1–16.

Beck, Nathaniel, and Jonathan N. Katz. 1995. "What to Do (and Not to Do) with Time-Series Cross-Section Data." *The American Political Science Review* 89 (3): 634–647. doi:10.2307/2082979.

Berman, Eli, John Bound, and Zvi Griliches. 1994. "Changes in the Demand for Skilled Labor Within US Manufacturing: Evidence from the Annual Survey of Manufactures." *Quarterly Journal of Economics* 109 (2): 367–397.

Bernard, Andrew B., J. Bradford Jensen, and Peter K. Schott. 2009. "Importers, Exporters and Multinationals: A Portrait of Firms in the U.S. That Trade Goods." In *Producer Dynamics: New Evidence from Micro Data*, ed. Timothy Dunne, J. Bradford Jensen, and Mark J. Roberts, pp. 513–552. Chicago: University of Chicago Press.

Bernard, Andrew B., J. Bradford Jensen, Stephen J. Redding, and Peter K. Schott. 2012. "The Empirics of Firm Heterogeneity and International Trade." *Annual Review of Economics* 4: 283–313.

Bernard, Andrew, J. Bradford Jensen, Stephen J. Redding, and Peter K. Schott. 2010. Intra-Firm Trade and Product Contractability." *American Economic Review* 100(2): 444–448.

Bertrand, Marianne, Paras Mehta, and Sendhil Mullainathan. 2002. "Ferreting Out Tunneling: An Application to Indian Business Groups." *Quarterly Journal of Economics* 117 (1): 121–148.

Beugelsdijk, Sjoerd, Jean-François Hennart, Arjen Slangen, and Roger Smeets. 2010. "Why and How FDI Stocks Are a Biased Measure of MNE Affiliate Activity." *Journal of International Business Studies* 41 (9): 1444–1459. doi:10.1057/jibs.2010.29.

Bhagwati, Jagdish N., Elias Dinopoulos, and Kar-yu Wong. 1992. "Quid Pro Quo Foreign Investment." *American Economic Review* 82 (2): 186–190.

Blomström, Magnus, and Frederik Sjöholm. 1999. "Technology Transfer with Spillovers." *European Economic Review* 43: 915–923.

Blonigen, Bruce A., Ronald B. Davies, and Keith Head. 2003. "Estimating the Knowledge-Capital Model of the Multinational Enterprise: Comment." *American Economic Review* 93 (3): 980–1001.

Blonigen, Bruce A., and Robert C. Feenstra. 1996. "Protectionist Threats and Foreign Direct Investment." *NBER Working Paper* (5475).

Blonigen, Bruce A., and David M. Figlio. 1998. "Voting for Protection: Does Direct Foreign Investment Influence Legislator Behavior?" *American Economic Review* 88 (4): 1002–1014.

Blonigen, Bruce A., and Matthew J. Slaughter. 2002. "Foreign Affiliate Activity and US Skill Upgrading." *The Review of Economics and Statistics* 83 (2): 362–376.

Blonigen, Bruce A., KaSaundra Tomlin, and Wesley W. Wilson. 2004. "Tariff-Jumping FDI and Domestic Firms' Profits." *Canadian Journal of Economics* 37: 656–677.

Blonigen, Bruce A., and Miao Wang. 2004. "Inappropriate Pooling of Wealthy and Poor Countries in Empirical FDI Studies." *NBER Working Paper* (10378).

Borensztein, Eduardo, Jose De Gregorio, and Jong-Wha Lee. 1998. "How Does Foreign Direct Investment Affect Economic Growth?" *Journal of International Economics* 45 (1): 115–135.

Bradley, David G. 1977. "Managing against Expropriation." *Harvard Business Review* 55 (4): 75–83.

Brainard, S. Lael. 1997. "An Empirical Assessment of the Proximity-Concentration Trade-off Between Multinational Sales and Trade." *American Economic Review* 87 (4): 520–544.

Branstetter, Lee G, and Robert C Feenstra. 2002. "Trade and Foreign Direct Investment in China: a Political Economy Approach." *Journal of International Economics* 58: 335–358.

Branstetter, Lee, and Nicholas Lardy. 2006. "China's Embrace of Globalization." *National Bureau of Economic Research Working Paper Series* No. 12373. http://www.nber.org/papers/w12373

Breton, Albert. 1964. "The Economics of Nationalism." *Journal of Political Economy* 72 (4): 376–386.

Brock, William A., and Stephen P. Magee. 1978. "The Economics of Special Interest Politics: The Case of the Tariff." *The American Economic Review* 68 (2): 246–250.

Brock, William A., Stephen P. Magee, and Leslie Young. 1989. *Black Hole Tariffs and Endogenous Political Theory.* Cambridge: Cambridge University Press.

Brown, Drusilla K., Alan V. Deardorff, and Robert M. Stern. 2003. "The Effect of Multinational Production on Wages and Working Conditions in Developing Countries." *NBER Working Paper* (9669).

Brown, Drusilla K., and Robert M. Stern. 2001. "Measurement and Modeling of the Economic Effects of Trade and Investment Barriers in Services." *Review of International Economics* 9 (2): 262–286.

Budd, John W., Jozef Konings, and Matthew J. Slaughter. 2005. "Wages and International Rent Sharing in Multinational Firms." *Review of Economics & Statistics* 87 (1): 73–84. doi:10.1162/0034653053327586.

Burgoon, Brian, and Michael J. Hiscox. 2008. "The Gender Divide over International Trade: Why Do Men and Women Have Different Views About Openness to the World Economy?" *Harvard University Working Paper*.

Bustos, Paula. 2011. "Trade Liberalization, Exports, and Technology Upgrading: Evidence on the Impact of MERCOSUR on Argentinian Firms." *American Economic Review* 101 (1): 304–340. doi:10.1257/aer.101.1.304.

Büthe, Tim, and Helen V. Milner. 2008. "The Politics of Foreign Direct Investment into Developing Countries: Increasing FDI through International Trade Agreements?" *American Journal of Political Science* 52 (4): 741–762.

Cao, Xun, and Aseem Prakash. 2010. "Trade Competition and Domestic Pollution: A Panel Study, 1980–2003." *International Organization* 64 (3): 481–503. doi:10.1017/S0020818310000123.

Carr, David L., James R. Markusen, and Keith E. Maskus. 2001. "Competition for Multinational Investment in Developing Countries: Human Capital, Infrastructure and Market Size." In *CEPR/NBER/SNS Conference, International Seminar on International Trade: Challenges to Globalization.*

2003. "Estimating the Knowledge-Capital Model of the Multinational Enterprise: Reply." *The American Economic Review* 93 (3): 995–1001.

Caves, Richard E. 1971. "International Corporations: The Industrial Economics of Foreign Investment." *Economica* 38: 1–27.

Chandler, Alfred Dupont. 1962. *Strategy and Structure: Chapters in the History of the American Industrial Enterprise.* Beard Books.

Chang, Ha-Joon. 2004. "Regulation of Foreign Investment in Historical Perspective." *European Journal of Development Research* 16: 687–715.

Chari, Anusha, and Nandini Gupta. 2008. "Incumbents and Protectionism: The Political Economy of Foreign Entry Liberalization." *Journal of Financial Economics* 88 (3): 633–656. doi:10.1016/j.jfineco.2007.07.006.

Cheibub, José Antonio, Jennifer Gandhi, and James Raymond Vreeland. 2009. "Democracy and Dictatorship Revisited." *Public Choice* 143 (1–2): 67–101. doi:10.1007/s11127-009-9491-2.

Cheng, Tun-jen, and Stephan Haggard. 1987. *Newly Industrializing Asia in Transition.* Berkeley: Institute of International Studies, University of California.

Chung, Wilbur, W. Mitchell, and B. Yeung. 2003. "Foreign Direct Investment and Host Country Productivity: The American Automotive Component Industry in the 1980s." *Journal of International Business Studies* 34 (2): 199–218.

Cling, Jean-Pierre, Mireille Razafindrakoto, and François Roubaud. 2005. "Export Processing Zones in Madagascar: a Success Story Under Threat?" *World Development* 33 (5): 785–803. doi:10.1016/j.worlddev.2005.01.007.

Collier, Ruth Berins, and James Mahoney. 1997. "Adding Collective Actors to Collective Outcomes: Labor and Recent Democratization in South America and Southern Europe." *Comparative Politics* 29 (3): 285–303.

Crystal, Jonathan. 2003a. *Unwanted Company: Foreign Investment in American Industries.* Ithaca, NY: Cornell University Press.

2003b. "Bargaining in the Negotiations over Liberalizing Trade in Services: Power, Reciprocity, and Learning." *Review of International Political Economy* 10 (3): 552–578.

Cukierman, Alex, and Mariano Tomassi. 1998. "When Does It Take a Nixon to Go to China?" *American Economic Review* 88 (March): 180–197.

Deardorff, Alan V., and Robert M. Stern. 1998. *Measurement of Nontariff Barriers.* Ann Arbor: University of Michigan Press.

Desai, Mihir, C. Fritz Foley, and James R. Hines, Jr. 2004. "Capital Controls, Liberalizations, and Foreign Direct Investment." *NBER Working Paper* (10337).

Dollar, David, Mary Hallward-Driemeier, and Taye Mengistae. 2006. "Investment Climate and International Integration." *World Development* 34 (9): 1498–1516.

Domiguez, Jorge I. 1982. "Business Nationalism: Latin American National Business Attitudes and Behavior toward Multinational Enterprises." In *Economic Issues and Political Conflict: US–Latin American Relations*, ed. Jorge I. Domiguez, 16–68. London: Butterworth Scientific.

Dorobantu, Sinziana Paulina Ruxandra. 2011. "Political Competition and the Regulation of Foreign Direct Investment." http://dukespace.lib.duke.edu/dspace/handle/10161/2407.

Dunne, Timothy, J. Bradford Jensen, and Mark J. Roberts. 2009. *Producer Dynamics: New Evidence from Micro Data.* Chicago: University of Chicago Press.

Eichengreen, Barry, and David Leblang. 2008. "Democracy and Globalization." *Economics & Politics* 20 (3): 289–334. doi:10.1111/j.1468–0343.2007.00329.x.

Elkins, Zachary, Andrew T. Guzman, and Beth A. Simmons. 2006. "Competing for Capital: The Diffusion of Bilateral Investment Treaties, 1960–2000." *International Organization* 60 (4): 811–846. doi:10.1017/S0020818306060279.

Encarnation, Dennis J., and Louis T. Wells, Jr. 1985. "Sovereignty En Garde: Negotiating with Foreign Investors." *International Organization* 39 (1): 47–78.

Ethier, Wilfred. 1986. "The Multinational Firm." *Quarterly Journal of Economics* 101: 805–833.

Ethier, Wilfred, and James R. Markusen. 1996. "Multinationals, Technical Diffusion, and Trade." *Journal of International Economics* 41: 1–28.

Evans, Peter B. 1979. *Dependent Development: The Alliance of Multinational, State, and Local Capital in Brazil.* Princeton, NJ: Princeton University Press.

Evans, Peter, and Gary Gereffi. 1981. "Transnational Corporations, Dependent Development, and State Policy in the Semiperiphery: A Comparison of Brazil and Mexico." *Latin American Research Review* 16 (3): 31–64.

Faccio, Mara. 2006. "Politically Connected Firms." *The American Economic Review* 96 (March): 369–386. doi:10.1257/000282806776157704.

Fayerweather, John. 1982. "Elite Attitudes About Multinational Firms." In *Host National Attitudes toward Multinational Corporations*, ed. John Fayerweather, 1–43. New York: Praeger.

Feenstra, Robert C., and Gordon H. Hanson. 1997. "Foreign Direct Investment and Relative Wages: Evidence from Mexico's Maquiladoras." *Journal of International Economics* 42: 371–393.

Fernandez, Raquel, and Dani Rodrik. 1991. "Resistance to Reform: Status Quo Bias in the Presence of Individual- Specific Uncertainty." *The American Economic Review* 81 (5): 1146–1155. doi:10.2307/2006910.

Fields, Karl. 1997. "Strong States and Business Organization in Korea and Taiwan." In *Business and State in Developing Countries*, ed. Sylvia Maxfield and Ben R. Schneider, 122–150. Ithaca, NY: Cornell University Press.

Fisman, Raymond. 2001. "Estimating the Value of Political Connections." *The American Economic Review* 91 (4): 1095–1102.

Frieden, Jeffry A. 1991. "Invested Interests: The Politics of National Economic Policies in a World of Global Finance." *International Organization* 45 (4): 425–451.

Frieden, Jeffry A. 2006. *Global Capitalism: Its Fall and Rise in the Twentieth Century.* New York: W. W. Norton.

Froot, Kenneth A., and Jeremy C. Stein. 1991. "Exchange Rates and Foreign Direct Investment: An Imperfect Capital Markets Approach." *Quarterly Journal of Economics* 106 (4): 1191–1217.

Gallagher, Mary Elizabeth. 2007. *Contagious Capitalism.* Princeton, NJ: Princeton University Press.

Gatignon, Hubert, and Erin Anderson. 1988. "The Multinational Corporation's Degree of Control over Foreign Subsidiaries: An Empirical Test of a Transaction Cost Explanation." *Journal of Law, Economics, & Organization* 4 (2): 305–336.

Gilligan, Michael J. 1997. "Lobbying as a Private Good with Intra-Industry Trade." *International Studies Quarterly* 41 (3): 455–474.

Golub, Stephen S. 2003. "Measures of Restrictions on Inward Foreign Direct Investment for OCED Countries." *OECD Economics Department Working Paper* (ECO/WKP(2003)11).

Gomes-Casseres, Benjamin. 1990. "Firm Ownership Preferences and Host Government Restrictions: An Integrated Approach." *Journal of International Business Studies* First Quarter: 1–22.

Goodman, John B., Deborah L. Spar, and David B. Yoffie. 1996. "Foreign Direct Investment and the Demand for Protection." *International Organization* 50 (4): 555–591.

Görg, Holger, and David Greenway. 2001. "Foreign Direct Investment and Intra-Industry Spillovers: A Review of the Literature." *Globalisation and Labour Markets Programme, University of Nottingham* 2001/37.

Graham, Edward M., and Paul R. Krugman. 1995. *Foreign Direct Investment in the United States.* 3rd ed. Washington, DC: Institute for International Economics.

Graham, Edward M., and David M. Marchick. 2006. *US National Security and Foreign Direct Investment.* Washington, DC: Institute for International Economics.

Granovetter, Mark. 1995. "Coase Revisited: Business Groups in the Modern Economy." *Industrial and Corporate Change* 4 (1): 93 –130. doi:10.1093/icc/4.1.93.

Grieco, Joseph M. 1982. "Between Dependency and Autonomy: India's Experience with the International Computer Industry." *International Organization* 36 (3): 609–632.

Grossman, Gene M., and Elhanan Helpman. 1996. "Foreign Investment and Endogenous Protection." In *The Political Economy of Trade Policy: Papers in Honor of Jagdish Bhagwati*, ed. Robert C. Feenstra, Gene M. Grossman, and Douglas A. Irwin, pp. 199–224. Cambridge, MA: MIT Press.

Grossman, Sanford J., and Oliver D. Hart. 1986. "The Costs and Benefits of Ownership: A Theory of Vertical and Lateral Integration." *Journal of Political Economy* 94 (4): 691–719.

Grunwald, Joseph, and Kenneth Flamm. 1985. *The Global Factory: Foreign Assembly in International Trade.* Washington, DC: Brookings Institution Press.

Guadalupe, Maria, Olga Kuzmina, and Catherine Thomas. 2012. "Innovation and Foreign Ownership." *American Economic Review* 102 (7): 3594–3627.

Guillén, Mauro F. 2000a. "Organized Labor's Images of Multinational Enterprise: Divergent Foreign Investment Ideologies in Argentina, South Korea, and Spain." *Industrial and Labor Relations Review* 53 (3): 419–442.

2000b. "Business Groups in Emerging Economies: A Resource-Based View." *The Academy of Management Journal* 43 (3): 362–380. doi:10.2307/1556400.

Haddad, Mona, and Ann Harrison. 1993. "Are There Spillovers from Direct Foreign Investment? Evidence from Panel Data for Morocco." *Journal of Development Economics* 42: 51–74.

Haggard, Stephan. 1990. *Pathways from the Periphery.* Ithaca, NY: Cornell University Press.

Haggard, Stephan, and Robert R. Kaufman. 1995. *The Political Economy of Democratic Transitions.* Princeton, NJ: Princeton University Press.

Hainmueller, Jens, and Michael J. Hiscox. 2006. "Learning to Love Globalization: Education and Individual Attitudes Toward International Trade." *International Organization* 60 (2): 469–498. doi:10.1017/S0020818306060140.

2007. "Educated Preferences: Explaining Attitudes Toward Immigration in Europe." *International Organization* 61 (2): 399–442. doi:10.1017/S0020818307070142.

Hallward-Driemeier, Mary. 2003. "Do Bilateral Investment Treaties Attract FDI? Only a Bit … and They Could Bite." World Bank Working Paper 3121.

Hanson, Gordon H., Raymond J. Mataloni, and Matthew J. Slaughter. 2001. "Expansion Strategies of Multinational Firms." *NBER Working Paper* (8433).

2003. "Vertical Production Networks in Multinational Firms." *NBER Working Paper* (9723).

Hardin, Alexis, and Leanne Holmes. 2000. "Assessing Barriers to Service Sector Investment." In *Impediments to Trade in Services: Measurement and Policy Implications*, ed. Christopher Findlay and Tony Warren, 52–70. London: Routledge.

Harrison, Ann. 1996. "Determinants and Effects of Direct Foreign Investment in Cote d'Ivoire, Morocco, and Venezuela." In *Industrial Evolution in Developing Countries*, ed. Mark J Roberts and James R Tybout, 163–183. Oxford: Oxford UP/World Bank.

Helpman, Elhanan. 1984. "A Simple Theory of Multinational Corporations." *Journal of Political Economy* 92: 451–471.

2006. "Trade, FDI, and the Organization of Firms." *Journal of Economic Literature* 44 (3): 589–630.

Helpman, Elhanan, and Paul R. Krugman. 1985. *Market Structure and Foreign Trade.* Cambridge, MA: MIT Press.

Helpman, Elhanan, Marc J. Melitz, and Stephen R. Yeaple. 2004. "Export versus FDI with Heterogeneous Firms." *American Economic Review* 94: 300–316.

Henisz, Witold. 2000. "The Institutional Environment for Multinational Investment." *Journal of Law & Economics in Organizations* 16 (2): 334–364. doi:10.1093/jleo/16.2.334.

2002. *Politics and International Investment: Measuring Risks and Protecting Profits.* Cheltham: Edward Elgar.

Henisz, Witold, and Oliver Williamson. 1999. "*Comparative Economic Organizations – within and between Countries.*" *Business and Politics* 1 (3): 261–277.

Henisz, Witold J., and Bennet A. Zelner. 2005. "Legitimacy, Interest Group Pressures, and Change in Emergent Institutions: The Case of Foreign Investors and Host Country Governments." *Academy of Management Review* 30 (2): 361–382.

Hines, Jr., James R. 1995. "Taxes, Technology Transfer, and R&D by Multinational Firms." In *Taxing Multinational Corporations*, ed. Martin Feldstein, James R. Hines, Jr., and Glenn Hubbard. Chicago: University of Chicago Press.

Hiscox, Michael J. 2002. "Commerce, Coalitions, and Factor Mobility." *American Political Science Review* 96 (3): 593–608.

2004. "International Capital Mobility and Trade Politics: Capital Flows, Political Coalitions, and Lobbying." *Economics and Politics* 16 (3): 253–285.

2006. "Through a Glass and Darkly: Attitudes toward International Trade and the Curious Effects of Issue Framing." *International Organization* 60 (3): 755–780. doi:10.1017/S0020818306060255.

Horstmann, Ignatius, and James R. Markusen. 1987. "Strategic Investments and the Development of Multinationals." *International Economic Review* 28: 109–121.

Huang, Yasheng. 2003. *Selling China: Foreign Direct Investment During the Reform Era.* Cambridge: Cambridge University Press.

Hummels, David, Jun Ishii, and Kei-Mu Yi. 2001. "The Nature and Growth of Vertical Specialization in World Trade." *Journal of International Economics* 54 (1): 75–96. doi:10.1016/S0022–1996(00)00093–3.

Huntington, Samuel. 1991. *The Third Wave: Democratization in the Late Twentieth Century.* Norman: University of Oklahma Press.

Hymer, Stephen. 1976. *The International Operations of National Firms.* Cambridge, MA: MIT Press.

Irwin, Douglas A. 1994. "The Political Economy of Free Trade: Voting in the British General Election of 1906." *Journal of Law and Economics* 37 (1): 75–108.

1996. "The United States in a New Global Economy? A Century's Perspective." *The American Economic Review* 86 (2): 41–46.

Jaggers, Keith, and Monty G. Marshall. 2004. *Polity IV Project. Integrated Network for Societal Conflict Research Program and Center for International Development and Conflict Management.*

Javorcik, Beata S., and Mariana Spatareanu. 2011. "Does It Matter Where You Come From? Vertical Spillovers from Foreign Direct Investment and the Origin of Investors." *Journal of Development Economics* 96 (1): 126–138. doi:10.1016/j.jdeveco.2010.05.008.

Javorcik, Beata Smarzynska. 2004. "Does Foreign Direct Investment Increase the Productivity of Domestic Firms? In Search of Spillovers through Backward Linkages." *The American Economic Review* 94 (3): 605–627. doi:10.1257/0002828041464605.

Javorcik, Beata Smarzynska, and Shang-Jin Wei. 2000. "Corruption and the Composition of FDI." *World Bank Working Paper* WPS2360.

Jensen, Nathan. 2008. "Political Risk, Democratic Institutions, and Foreign Direct Investment." *The Journal of Politics* 70 (4): 1040–1052. doi:10.1017/S0022381608081048.

Jensen, Nathan et al. 2012. *Politics and Foreign Direct Investment.* Ann Arbor: University of Michigan Press.

Jensen, Nathan M. 2003. "Democratic Governance and Multinational Corporations: Political Regimes and Inflows of Foreign Direct Investment." *International Organization* 57 (3): 587–616.

Jensen, Nathan Michael. 2006. *Nation-States and the Multinational Corporation: A Political Economy of Foreign Direct Investment.* Princeton, NJ: Princeton University Press

Jodice, David A. 1980. "Sources of Change in Third World Regimes for Foreign Direct Investment. 1968–1976." *International Organization* 34 (2): 177–206.

Johnston, Barry R, Mark Swinburne, Alexander Kyei, Bernard Laurens, David Mitchem, Inci Otker, Susana Sosa, and Natalia Tamirisa. 1999. *Exchange Rate Arrangements and Currency Convertability: Developments and Issues.* Washington, DC: International Monetary Fund.

Jones, Geoffrey. 2005. *Renewing Unilever: Transformation And Tradition.* Oxford: Oxford University Press.

Jones, Ronald W. 1971. "A Three-Factor Model in Theory, Trade, and History." In *Trade, Balance of Payments, and Growth,* ed. Jagdish N. Bhagwati, Ronald W. Jones, Robert A. Mundell, and Jaroslav Vanek, 3–21. New York: American Elsevier Publishing Company.

Kang, Eliot C. S. 1997. "U.S. Politics and Greater Regulation of Inward Foreign Direct Investment." *International Organization* 51 (2): 301–333.

Kaufman, Robert R., and Leo Zuckermann. 1998. "Attitudes toward Economic Reform in Mexico: The Role of Political Orientations." *The American Political Science Review* 92 (2): 359–375. doi:10.2307/2585669.

Keller, Wolfgang, and Stephen Yeaple. 2009. "Multinational Enterprises, International Trade, and Technology Diffusion: A Firm-level Evidence the United States," *Review of Economics and Statistics* 91 (4): 821–831.

Keohane, Robert O., and Van Doorn Ooms. 1975. "The Multinational Firm and International Regulation." *International Organization* 29 (1): 169–209.

Khanna, Tarun, and Yishay Yafeh. 2007. "Business Groups in Emerging Markets: Paragons or Parasites?" *Journal of Economic Literature* 45 (2): 331–372. doi:10.1257/jel.45.2.331.

Klein, Benjamin, Robert G. Crawford, and Armen A. Alchian. 1978. "Vertical Integration, Appropriable Rents, and the Competitive Contracting Process." *Journal of Law & Economics* 21: 297.

Knickerbocker, Fredrick T. 1973. *Oligopolistic Reaction and Multinational Enterprise.* Boston: Harvard Business School.

Kobrin, Stephen J. 1980. "Foreign Enterprise and Forced Investment in LDCs." *International Organization* 34 (1): 65–88.

———. 1987. "Testing The Bargaining Hypothesis in the Manufacturing Sector in Developing Countries." *International Organization* 41 (4): 609–638.

Kono, D. Y. 2008. "Democracy and Trade Discrimination." *Journal of Politics* 70 (4): 942–955. doi:10.1017/S0022381608080985.

Kono, Daniel. 2006. "Optimal Obfuscation: Democracy and Trade Policy Transparency." *American Political Science Review* 100 (3): 369–384. doi:10.1017/S0003055406062241.

Krasner, Stephen D. 1985. *Structural Conflict*. Berkeley: University of California Press.

Kucera, David. 2002. "Core Labour Standards and Foreign Direct Investment." *International Labour Review* 141: 31–69.

La Porta, Rafael, Florencio Lopez-de-Silanes, and Andrei Shleifer. 1998. "Corporate Ownership Around the World." *Working Papers – Yale School of Management's Economics Research Network* (January): 1. doi:Working Paper.

Lane, Philip R., and Gian Maria Milesi-Ferretti. 2007. "The External Wealth of Nations Mark II: Revised and Extended Estimates of Foreign Assets and Liabilities, 1970–2004." *Journal of International Economics* 73 (2): 223–250.

Leblang, David, and Shanker Satyanath. 2008. "Politically Generated Uncertainty and Currency Crises: Theory, Tests, and Forecasts." *Journal of International Money and Finance* 27 (3): 480–497. doi:10.1016/j.jimonfin.2008.01.006.

Levinsohn, James. 1997. "Carwars: Trying to Make Sense of US-Japan Trade Frictions in the Automobile and Automobile Parts Industry." In *The Effects of US Trade Protection and Promotion Policies*, ed. Robert C. Feenstra, 11–32. Chicago: University of Chicago Press/NBER.

Li, Quan. 2009. "Democracy, Autocracy, and Expropriation of Foreign Direct Investment." *Comparative Political Studies* 42(8): 1098–1127.

Li, Quan, and Adam Resnick. 2003. "Reversal of Fortunes: Democracy, Property Rights and Foreign Direct Investment Inflows to Developing Countries." *International Organization* 57 (1): 175–211.

Lipsey, Robert. 2002. "Home and Host Country Effects of FDI." *NBER Working Paper* (9292).

Lipsey, Robert, and Frederik Sjöholm. 2002. "Foreign Firms and Indonesian Manufacturing Wages: An Analysis With Panel Data." *NBER Working Paper* (9417).

Mansfield, Edward D., and Diana C. Mutz. 2009. "Support for Free Trade: Self-Interest, Sociotropic Politics, and Out-Group Anxiety." *International Organization* 63 (3): 425–457. doi:10.1017/S0020818309090158.

Markusen, James R. 1984. "Multinationals, Multi-plant Economies, and the Gains from Trade." *Journal of International Economics* 16: 205–226.

Markusen, James R., and Keith E. Maskus. 2001. "General Equilibrium Approaches to the Multinational Firm: A Review of Theory and Practice." *NBER Working Paper* (8334).

Mataloni, Raymond J. 1995. "A Guide to BEA Statistics on US Multinational Companies." *Survey of Current Business*: 38–55.

Mayda, Anna Maria. 2006. "Who Is Against Immigration? A Cross-Country Investigation of Individual Attitudes toward Immigrants." *Review of Economics and Statistics* 88 (3): 510–530.

Mayda, Anna Maria, and Dani Rodrik. 2005. "Why Are Some People (and Countries) More Protectionist Than Others?" *European Economic Review* 49 (6): 1393–1430. doi:10.1016/j.euroecorev.2004.01.002.

Melitz, Marc J. 2003. "The Impact of Trade on Intra-Industry Reallocations and Aggregate Industry Productivity." *Econometrica* 71: 1695–1725.

Mesquita, Bruce Bueno de, Alastair Smith, Randolph M. Siverson, and James D. Morrow. 2004. *The Logic of Political Survival*. Cambridge, MA: The MIT Press.

Milner, Helen V. 1988. "Trading Places: Industries for Free Trade." *World Politics* 40 (3): 350–376.

Milner, Helen V., and Keiko Kubota. 2005. "Why the Move to Free Trade? Democracy and Trade Policy in the Developing Countries." *International Organization* 59 (1): 107–143.

Milner, Helen V., and Bumba Mukherjee. 2009. "Democratization and Economic Globalization." *Annual Review of Political Science* 12 (1): 163–181. doi:10.1146/annurev.polisci.12.110507.114722.

Minor, Michael S. 1994. "The Demise of Expropriation as an Instrument of LDC Policy, 1980–1992." *Journal of International Business Studies* 25 (1): 177–188.

Mitra, Devashish, Dimitrios D Thomakos, and Mehmet A Ulubasogflu. 2002. "'Protection for Sale' in a Developing Country: Democracy Versus Dictatorship." *Review of Economics and Statistics* 84 (3): 497–508.

Mitton, Todd. 2008. "Institutions and Concentration." *Journal of Development Economics* 86 (2): 367–394. doi:10.1016/j.jdeveco.2007.10.001.

Monteverde, Kirk, and David J Teece. 1982. "Supplier Switching Costs and Vertical Integration in the Automobile Industry." *Bell Journal of Economics* 13 (1): 206–213.

Moran, Theodore H. 1998. *Foreign Direct Investment and Development: A New Policy Agenda for Developing Countries and Economies in Transition*. Washington DC: Institute for International Economics.

___ 2002. *Beyond Sweatshops: Foreign Direct Investment and Globalization in Developing Countries*. Washington, DC: Brookings Institution Press.

Morck, Randall, Daniel Wolfenzon, and Bernard Yeung. 2005. "Corporate Governance, Economic Entrenchment, and Growth." *Journal of Economic Literature* 43 (3): 655–720.

Mosley, Layna. 2010. *Labor Rights and Multinational Production*. Cambridge: Cambridge University Press.

Mukherjee, Arijit, and Kullapat Suetrong. 2009. "Privatization, Strategic Foreign Direct Investment and Host-Country Welfare." *European Economic Review* 53 (7): 775–785. doi:10.1016/j.euroecorev.2009.02.004.

Mullainathan, Sendhil, Paras Mehta, and Marianne Bertrand. 2002. "Ferreting Out Tunneling: An Application to Indian Business Groups." *Quarterly Journal of Economics* 117 (1): 121–148.

Murillo, Maria Victoria. 2001. *Labor Unions, Partisan Coalitions, and Market Reforms in Latin America*. Cambridge: Cambridge University Press.

Murtha, Thomas P. 1991. "Surviving Industrial Targeting: State Credibility and Public Policy Contingencies in Multinational Subcontracting." *Journal of Law, Economics, & Organization* 7 (1): 117–143.

Mussa, Michael. 1974. "Tariffs and the Distribution of Income." *Journal of Political Economy* 82: 1191–1204.

Naoi, Megumi, and Ikuo Kume. 2011. "Explaining Mass Support for Agricultural Protectionism: Evidence from a Survey Experiment During the Global Recession." *International Organization* 65 (4): 771–795. doi:10.1017/S0020818311000221.

Neary, J. Peter. 1978. "Short-Run Capital Specificity and the Pure Theory of International Trade." *The Economic Journal* 88 (351): 488–510. doi:10.2307/2232049.

Nicoletti, Giuseppe, Stephen S. Golub, Dana Hajkova, Daniel Mirza, and Kwang-Yeol Yoo. 2003. "Policies and International Integration: Influences on Trade and Foreign Direct Investment." *OECD Economics Department Working Paper* (ECO/WKP(2003)13).

Nunn, Nathan. 2007. "Relationship-Specificity, Incomplete Contracts, and the Pattern of Trade." *The Quarterly Journal of Economics* 122 (2): 569 –600. doi:10.1162/qjec.122.2.569.

O'Rourke, Kevin H., and Richard Sinnott. 2001. "The Determinants of Individual Trade Policy Preferences: International Survey Evidence [with Comments and Discussion]." *Brookings Trade Forum*: 157–206. doi:10.2307/25063160.

Oldenski, Lindsay. 2012. "Export Versus FDI and the Communication of Complex Information." *Journal of International Economics* 87(2): 312–322.

Oman, Charles. 2000. *Policy Competition for Foreign Direct Investment: A Study of Competition Among Governments to Attract FDI.* Paris: OECD Publishing.

Owen, Erica. forthcoming. "Unionization and Restrictions on Foreign Direct Investment," *International Interactions.*

Oxfam. 2007. "Signing Away the Future." *Oxfam Briefing Paper.*

Oxley, Joanne E. 1997. "Appropriability Hazards and Governance in Strategic Alliances: A Transaction Cost Approach." *Journal of Law & Economics in Organizations* 13 (2): 387–409.

Pauly, Louis W., and Simon Reich. 1997. "National Structures and Multinational Corporate Behavior: Enduring Differences in the Age of Globalization." *International Organization* 51 (1): 1–30. doi:10.1162/002081897550285.

Pavcnik, Nina. 2002. "Trade Liberalization, Exit, and Productivity Improvements: Evidence from Chilean Plants." *Review of Economic Studies* 69: 245–276.

Pearson, Margaret M. 1991. *Joint Ventures in the People's Republic of China.* Princeton, NJ: Princeton University Press.

Pinto, Pablo M., and Santiago M. Pinto. 2008. "The Politics of Investment Partisanship and the Sectoral Allocation of Foreign Direct Investment." *Economics & Politics* 20 (2): 216–254. doi:10.1111/j.1468–0343.2008.00330.x.

Portes, Richard, and Hélène Rey. 2005. "The Determinants of Cross-Border Equity Flows." *Journal of International Economics* 65 (2): 269–296. doi:10.1016/j.jinteco.2004.05.002.

Quinn, Dennis, and Carla Inclan. 1997. "The Origins of Financial Liberalization: A Study of Current and Capital Account Liberalization." *American Journal of Political Science* 41 (3): 771–813.

Rajan, Raghuram G., and Luigi Zingales. 2003. "The Great Reversals: The Politics of Financial Development in the Twentieth Century." *Journal of Financial Economics* 69 (1): 5–50. doi:10.1016/S0304–405X(03)00125–9.

Ramachandran, Vijaya. 1993. "Technology Transfer, Firm Ownership, and Investment in Human Capital." *The Review of Economics and Statistics* 75 (4): 664–670. doi:10.2307/2110020.

Rodrik, Dani. 1995. "Political Economy of Trade Policy." In *Handbook of International Economics*, ed. Gene M Grossman and Kenneth Rogoff, 3:1457–1494. Amsterdam: Elsevier.

    1996. "Understanding Economic Policy Reform." *Journal of Economic Literature* 34 (1): 9–41.

1999. "Democracies Pay Higher Wages." *Quarterly Journal of Economics* 114 (3): 707–738. doi:10.1162/003355399556115.

Rodrik, Dani, and Romain Wacziarg. 2005. "Do Democratic Transitions Produce Bad Economic Outcomes?" *The American Economic Review* 95 (2): 50–55.

Romer, Paul. 1993. "Idea Gaps and Object Gaps in Economic Development." *Journal of Monetary Economics* 32 (3): 543–573.

Sachs, Jeffrey D., and Andrew M. Warner. 1995. "Natural Resource Abundance and Economic Growth." *National Bureau of Economic Research Working Paper Series* No. 5398. http://www.nber.org/papers/w5398.

Sauvant, Karl P. 2009. "FDI Protectionism Is on the Rise." *World Bank* (September). https://openknowledge.worldbank.org/handle/10986/4244.

Scheve, Kenneth, and Matthew J. Slaughter. 2001a. "Labor Market Competition and Individual Preferences Over Immigration Policy." *Review of Economics and Statistics* 83 (1): 133–145.

2004. "Economic Insecurity and the Globalization of Production." *American Journal of Political Science* 48 (4): 662–674. doi:10.1111/j.0092–5853.2004.00094.x.

Scheve, Kenneth F., and Matthew J. Slaughter. 2001b. "What Determines Individual Trade Policy Preferences?" *Journal of International Economics* 54 (2): 267–292.

Schindler, Martin. 2009. "Measuring Financial Integration: A New Data Set." *IMF Staff Papers* 56 (1): 222–238.

Schmalensee, Richard. 1989. "Inter-Industry Studies of Structure and Performance." In *Handbook of Industrial Organization, Volume 2*, eds. Richard Schmalensee and Robert D WIllig. Amsterdam: Elsevier.

Sembenelli, Alessandro, and Georges Siotis. 2008. "Foreign Direct Investment and Mark-up Dynamics: Evidence from Spanish Firms." *Journal of International Economics* 76 (1): 107–115. doi:10.1016/j.jinteco.2008.05.003.

Servan-Schreiber, J. J. 1967. *The American Challenge.* New York: Atheneum.

Siegel, Jordan. 2007. "Contingent Political Capital and International Alliances: Evidence from South Korea." *Administrative Science Quarterly* 52 (4): 621–666.

Simmons, Beth A., and Zachary Elkins. 2004. "The Globalizaion of Liberalization: Policy Diffusion in the International Political Economy." *American Political Science Review* 98 (1): 171–189.

Stock, James H., and Motohiro Yogo. 2002. *Testing for Weak Instruments in Linear IV Regression.* National Bureau of Economic Research, Inc. http://ideas.repec.org/p/nbr/nberte/0284.html.

Stokes, Susan C. 1996a. "Economic Reform and Public Opinion in Peru, 1990–1995." *Comparative Political Studies* 29 (5): 544–565. doi:10.1177/0010414096029005003.

1996b. "Public Opinion and Market Reforms:: The Limits of Economic Voting." *Comparative Political Studies* 29 (5): 499–519. doi:10.1177/0010414096029005001.

2001. *Mandates and Democracy: Neoliberalism by Surprise in Latin America.* Cambridge: Cambridge University Press.

Stopford, John M., and Louis T. Wells, Jr. 1972. *Managing the Multinational Enterprise.* New York: Basic Books.

Sugges, Jr., Peter R. 1982. "Beliefs about the Multinational Enterprise: A Factor Analytical Study of British, Canadian, French, and Mexican Elites." In *Host National Attitudes toward Multinational Corporations*, ed. John Fayerweather, 44–61. New York: Praeger.

Svedberg, Peter. 1978. "The Portfolio-Direct Composition of Private Foreign Investment in 1914 Revisited." *The Economic Journal* 88 (352): 763–777. doi:10.2307/2231977.

Svejnar, Jan, and Stephen C. Smith. 1984. "The Economics of Joint Ventures in Less Developed Countries." *The Quarterly Journal of Economics* 99 (1): 149–167.

Teichova, Alice, Maurice Lévy-Leboyer, and Helga Nussbaum. 1986. *Multinational Enterprise in Historical Perspective.* Cambridge and New York: Cambridge University Press.

Thomas, Catherine. 2011. "Too Many Products: Decentralized Decision Making in Multinational Firms." *American Economic Journal: Microeconomics* 3 (February): 280–306. doi:10.1257/mic.3.1.280.

Tobin, Jennifer L., and Marc L. Busch. 2010. "A BIT Is Better Than a Lot: Bilateral Investment Treaties and Preferential Trade Agreements." *World Politics* 62 (1): 1–42. doi:10.1017/S0043887109990190.

Tomz, Michael, Jason Wittenberg, and Gary King. 2003. *CLARIFY: Software for Interpreting and Presenting Statistical Results.* Version 2.1. Stanford University, University of Wisconsin, and Harvard University.

Trefler, Daniel. 1993. "International Factor Price Differences: Leontief Was Right!" *The Journal of Political Economy* 101 (6): 961–987.

Tybout, James R. 2003. "Plant- and Firm-Level Evidence on 'New' Trade Theories." In *Handbook of International Trade,.* ed. E. Kwan Choi and James Harrigan, 388–415. Oxford: Basil Blackwell.

UNCTAD. 2003. *World Investment Report 2003: Transnational Corporation and Export Competitiveness.* Geneva: United Nations.

2004. *World Investment Report 2004.* Geneva: United Nations.

2011. *World Investment Report 2011.* Geneva: United Nations.

2012. *World Investment Report 2012.* Geneva: United Nations.

U.S. Bureau of Economic Analysis (BEA). 1977. *1977 Benchmark Survey of U.S. Direct Investment Abroad.* Washington DC: US Department of Commerce.

1999. *1999 Benchmark Survey of U.S. Direct Investment Abroad.* Washington DC: US Department of Commerce.

Ver Beek, Kurt Alan. 2001. "Maquiladoras: Exploitation or Emancipation? An Overview of the Situation of Maquiladora Workers in Honduras." *World Development* 29 (9): 1553–1567. doi:10.1016/S0305–750X(01)00057–2.

Verlegh, Peeter W.J., and Jan-Benedict E.M. Steenkamp. 1999. "A Review and Meta-analysis of Country-of-origin Research." *Journal of Economic Psychology* 20 (5): 521–546.

Vernon, Raymond. 1971. *Sovereignty at Bay.* New York: Basic Books.

Wei, Shang-Jin. 2000. "Local Corruption and Global Capital Flows." *Brookings Papers on Economic Activity* 2: 303–354.

Weyland, Kurt Gerhard. 2002. *The Politics of Market Reform in Fragile Democracies: Argentina, Brazil, Peru, and Venezuela.* Princeton, NJ: Princeton University Press.

Wheeler, David, and Ashoka Mody. 1992. "International Investment Location Decisions : The Case of U.S. Firms." *Journal of International Economics* 33 (1–2): 57–76.

Wilkins, Mira. 1989. *The History of Foreign Investment in the United States to 1914.* Cambridge, MA: Harvard University Press.

2004. *The History of Foreign Investment in the United States, 1914–1945*. Cambridge, MA: Harvard University Press.

Williamson, Oliver E. 1973. "Markets and Hierarchies: Some Elementary Considerations." *The American Economic Review* 63 (2): 316–325.

World Bank. 2003a. *Global Development Finance: Stiving for Stability in Development Finance*. Washington, DC: World Bank.

2003b. *Private Participation in Infrastructure: Trends in Developing Countries, 1990–2001*. Washington, DC. World Bank.

2003c. *Global Development Finance, Volume 1*. Washington, DC: World Bank.

2005. *World Development Indicators*. Washington, DC: World Bank.

Yeaple, Stephen R. 2003. "The Role of Skill Endowments in the Structure of US Outward Foreign Direct Investment." *Review of Economics and Statistics* 85 (3): 726–734.

Yi, Kei-Mu. 2003. "Can Vertical Specialization Explain the Growth of World Trade?" *Journal of Political Economy* 111 (1): 52–102.

Yoffie, David. 1993. "Foreign Direct Investment in Semiconductors." In *Foreign Direct Investment.*, ed. Kenneth A. Froot, 197–230. Chicago: University of Chicago Press/NBER.

Young, Stephen, Neil Hood, and Jim Hamill. 1988. *Foreign Multinationals and the British Economy*. London: Routledge.

Index

advertising. *See* marketing
Antràs, Pol, 60
Argentina, 62, 74
  expropriation, 70–71
  labor unions, 46
asset specificity
  effect on FDI policy alignments, 37–38
Australia
  FDI regulation, 7

bilateral investment treaties (BITs), 10, 37, 98
  role in FDI regulation, 53, 142
Bolivia, 69, 74
brand. *See* marketing
Brazil, 4, 62, 74, 153, 157, 166
  export-oriented FDI, 61
  FDI incentives, 10
  FDI regulation, 132–36
Bureau of Economic Analysis United States
  (BEA)
  Survey of Direct Investment Abroad, 13,
    35–36, 113–17, 119, 127–28
business groups, 45, 61–62

Canada, 7, 12, 33, 36
capital controls, FDI and, 18, 36, 55, 144–45
China, 4, 52, 134–35, 143
colonial origin. *See also* diffusion, FDI
  liberalization
  role in FDI regulation, 98, 100
Committee on Foreign Investment in the
  United States, 57, 137
contracting risk, 25–29
corruption
  FDI, 53

democracy
  measurement of, 91, 100
democratization, 14, 89–90, 157, 160, 163
  role of labor unions, 46
diffusion, FDI liberalization, 98–100
Dubai
  FDI outflows, 137

economic crisis, 107
  banking, 96, 107
  currency, 96, 107
  FDI inflows following, 1, 41, 63–64
  FDI policymaking, 95–97
  sovereign debt, 96, 107
economies of scale, 5, 29, 34, 41, 132
  See wage premium: MNC employment
Europe
  opposition to FDI, 7
Evans, Peter. *See* triple alliance
export processing zones, 60, 73, 133
export-oriented FDI, 15, 31–36, 48, 109–10
expropriation, 8, 10, 18, 59–60

FDI, 33
  automobile industry, 7, 10, 26–27, 33–34,
    59, 137
  chemical industry, 6–7, 13, 62, 73
  computer hardware industry, 35, 110, 121
  consumer products industry, 5–6, 21, 57,
    135–36
  electronics industry, 7, 32–33
  historical patterns, 4–5, 36–37
  measurement of, 2, 17–18, 63, 133
  natural resources industry, 2, 56, 64, 69–71
  pharmaceutical industry, 6, 25, 28

Other Books in the Series (*continued from page iii*)